COLOSSIANS

— Rooted in Him —

KRISTIN SCHMUCKER

STUDY SUGGESTIONS

Thank you for choosing this study to help you dig into God's Word.
We are so passionate about men and women getting into Scripture, and we are
praying that this study will be a tool to help you do that.

———————

Here are a few tips to help you get the most from this study:

- Before you begin, take time to look into the context of the book. Find out who
  wrote it and learn about the cultural climate it was written in, as well as where
  it fits on the biblical timeline. Then take time to read through the entire book of
  the Bible we are studying if you are able. This will help you to get the big picture
  of the book and will aid in comprehension, interpretation, and application.

- Start your study time with prayer. Ask God to help you understand what you
  are reading and allow it to transform you (Psalm 119:18).

- Look into the context of the book as well as the specific passage.

- Before reading what is written in the study, read the assigned passage!
  Repetitive reading is one of the best ways to study God's Word. Read it
  several times, if you are able, before going on to the study. Read in several
  translations if you find it helpful.

- As you read the text, mark down observations and questions. Write down things
  that stand out to you, things that you notice, or things that you don't understand.
  Look up important words in a dictionary or interlinear Bible.

- Look for things like verbs, commands, and references to God. Notice key terms
  and themes throughout the passage.

- After you have worked through the text, read what is written in the study.
  Take time to look up any cross-references mentioned as you study.

- Then work through the questions provided in the book. Read and answer
  them prayerfully.

- Paraphrase or summarize the passage, or even just one verse from the passage. Putting it into your own words helps you to slow down and think through every word.

- Focus your heart on the character of God that you have seen in this passage. What do you learn about God from the passage you have studied? Adore Him and praise Him for who He is.

- Think and pray through application and how this passage should change you. Get specific with yourself. Resist the urge to apply the passage to others. Do you have sin to confess? How should this passage impact your attitude toward people or circumstances? Does the passage command you to do something? Do you need to trust Him for something in your life? How does the truth of the gospel impact your everyday life?

- We recommend you have a Bible, pen, highlighters, and journal as you work through this study. We recommend that ballpoint pens instead of gel pens be used in the study book to prevent smearing.

Here are several other optional resources
that you may find helpful as you study:

WWW.BLUELETTERBIBLE.ORG

This free website is a great resource for digging deeper. You can find translation comparison, an interlinear option to look at words in the original languages, Bible dictionaries, and even commentary.

A DICTIONARY

If looking up words in the Hebrew and Greek feels intimidating, look up words in English. Often times we assume we know the meaning of a word, but looking it up and seeing its definition can help us understand a passage better.

A DOUBLE-SPACED COPY OF THE TEXT

You can use a website like www.biblegateway.com to copy the text of a passage and print out a double-spaced copy to be able to mark on easily. Circle, underline, highlight, draw arrows, and mark in any way you would like to help you dig deeper and work through a passage.

TABLE *of* CONTENTS

JESUS *PLUS*
ANYTHING IS
NOT THE
MESSAGE *OF*
THE GOSPEL.

INTRODUCTION

Read Colossians 1–4

———

Jesus. Colossians points us to Jesus. This letter gives us a beautiful picture of our Savior and compels our hearts to worship and adoration. The book of Colossians fills our hearts with awe in the presence of the preeminent Christ, and it urges us to live our lives in light of our glorious union with Christ. Colossians is theological and practical. It points us to the character of God and to who we are in light of the truth of who He is.

The letter is written to the church at Colossae. The church was likely founded during Paul's missionary journeys, but not founded by Paul himself. Church history tells us that the church was founded and led by Epaphras. The letter was written by Paul to the Colossian church. Timothy is mentioned in the opening greeting as well and is regarded as most to be Paul's amanuensis which means secretary or assistant in writing. The letter was probably written during the same time period as Paul's letters to Philemon and the Ephesian church, and the book of Colossians bears a striking resemblance to the book of Ephesians.

The letter is written to a church that has begun to be infiltrated by false teaching. The false teaching came in subtly with a message that sounded appealing to the Colossian Christians. It was a message of Jesus plus _____. But Jesus plus anything is not the message of the gospel. Contrary to what trendy t-shirts and coffee mugs may tell us, we do not need Jesus and tacos or Jesus and coffee. We need Jesus.

In Colossians, Paul comes to build his case. Why is Jesus all that we need? Why is Jesus better? Why is Jesus preeminent? Why is Jesus sufficient? How does who Jesus is and what He has done change us? How should we live our lives in light of who Jesus is? Paul urges us to look to Jesus as the answer to every sorrow, every sin, and every situation. He pleads with us to live for the glory of God.

———

There are many themes in the book of Colossians. In it we find themes such as the gospel, union with Christ, and the Christian life. But if there was just one theme we could choose for this short book, it would the superiority and preeminence of Christ. Every verse points to Him and declares His praise. The goal of this letter is to lift high the name of Jesus. That is the goal of this study as well. And it should be the goal of every child of God.

- A DEEPER LOOK AT COLOSSIANS -

As you read the book of Colossians, note any key themes, words, or concepts and mark them below.

_____
_____
_____
_____
_____
_____
_____
_____
_____
_____
_____
_____
_____
_____
_____
_____
_____

IN CHRIST

Colossians 1:1-2

———

The book of Colossians is a letter to the church at Colossae. Though in our modern culture we typically include the information from the sender of the letter at the end, during the first century this information was included at the very beginning of the letter. So this letter to the Colossians begins by pointing us to Paul, the author of the letter.

It is in this initial greeting that we learn that the letter was written by Paul. Here, Paul is identified for us as an apostle of Christ Jesus. The word apostle literally means "sent one," and Paul identifies himself as one sent by Christ Jesus. The role of the apostle was a very important role in the early church as the apostles spoke and wrote with the authority of God as His delegates or representatives. Paul's statement of apostleship confirms his authority to write to the Colossians with instruction from God. We must not let the familiarity of the name Christ Jesus allow us to lose the radical statement that it was. The title "Christ" identified Jesus as the Messiah. He was the one who the world had been waiting for, and the one upon whom all Scripture is centered. Paul recognizes that his calling is by the will of God. He is not coming to the Colossians with his own message, but with gospel truth.

The greeting of Colossians is also where we see that Timothy had a role in the writing of this letter. He is typically thought to have been an assistant to Paul in writing, as the letter is full of personal singular pronouns. He is identified here as Timothy our brother. By using this language, Paul gives us a beautiful picture of the people of God as the family of God. In Christ, we are brothers and sisters knit together in an unbreakable familial bond.

The letter is written to the saints and the faithful brothers and sisters. The saints are those who believe in Jesus and the message of the gospel. The language calls our attention back to the people of Israel in the Old Testament described as a called-out people. The apostle Peter in 1 Peter 2:9 applies this same language to the people of God both Jew

———

and Gentile. The church is the holy people of God. They are the called-out ones and the saints. The church is the true spiritual Israel. Paul also speaks of his audience as faithful brothers and sisters. While this could be interpreted to mean that they are the faithful in the sense that they have placed faith in Christ, it seems more likely in the context that Paul is referring to them as faithful to the Lord and steadfast disciples.

Paul uses two prepositional phrases to identify his audience. He identifies them by their physical location at Colossae, but then he also points to their spiritual position. The people of God are in Christ. This small statement is one of the key themes of the entire book of Colossians and the entire New Testament. Believers are in Christ. By grace and through faith, He is in us, and we are in Him. We are secure in Him, and we now live through Him. This doctrine is essential to our understanding of the gospel and how to live the Christian life. Paul will talk more about this doctrine throughout the book of Colossians as he roots all of his theology in the fact that we are in Christ.

Paul ends his greeting with the traditional New Testament message of grace and peace. He desires for his readers to grow in the abundant grace of God. He desires for them to be mature believers walking with Christ, and he desires for them to live their lives with the peace of God permeating every aspect of their lives.

The book of Colossians opens with a greeting that would be easy for us to skip over, and yet even these introductory statements are inspired by God and contain truth that should stir our hearts with affection for Christ and a desire to walk in His grace.

We must not let the familiarity of the name Christ Jesus allow us to lose the radical statement that it was.

We could be tempted to skip the greeting and jump right into the text of the book, but what important insights can we gain from this greeting?

_____

_____

_____

_____

_____

_____

Paraphrase Colossians 1:1-2

_____

_____

_____

_____

_____

_____

Throughout the book of Colossians, Paul will reference our union with Christ. How does or *should* this doctrine change our daily living?

_____

_____

_____

_____

_____

_____

_____

_____

FAITH, LOVE,

AND *HOPE*

COME FROM

THE LORD.

FAITH, LOVE, HOPE

Colossians 1:3–5a

———

Paul moves into thanksgiving for the church at Colossae. This is a typical part of the greeting in the majority of his letters (all but Galatians). The words of thanksgiving are not mere formality, but are overflowing with rich doctrine that is applicable for our daily lives.

Paul begins the thanksgiving by telling the church at Colossae that he thanks God for them and prays for them constantly. He points to God as the Father of our Lord Jesus Christ. This is significant. In a book that will focus primarily on the person and work of Christ, Paul is careful to show the intimate nature of the trinitarian relationship by linking the Son with the Father. And though Jews before the time of Jesus did know that God is Father, His fatherhood was revealed to us in greater detail through the cross. It is through the Son and through the Spirit that we experience the initiating love of the Father.

As the greeting and thanksgiving continues, Paul speaks of what he knows about the Colossian Christians, and in doing so, he points to several of the marks of true disciples. Three traits are listed here: faith, love, and hope. References by Paul to these three things are common, and often found in conjunction with each other throughout the New Testament in passages such as 1 Corinthians 13:13 and 1 Thessalonians 1:3. These three qualities are not things that we possess on our own; they are works of the Spirit of God in us. Faith, love, and hope come from the Lord and not from anything in ourselves.

The first of these attributes is faith. The faith here is distinguished as faith in Christ. This is not about simply "having faith" in anything. It is about faith in Christ. In one way this references the object of our faith, which is Jesus Christ alone. This may also be referring, as in verse 2, to the location or position of our faith. We live in faith as we live in Christ through union with Him.

The next attribute that is listed is love. Specifically, this is love for the saints. The people of God should be marked by a supernatural love for one another. They are characterized by the bond of love that is present in the family of God. Paul has already reminded us that we are brothers and sisters, and now he points to the truth that as brothers and sisters we should love one another.

The final attribute listed is the one from which the others stem, and it is hope. Perhaps we would think that faith is the root. But Paul shows us a beautiful picture of hope as the center, and from there, our faith and Christian love flow. This hope is the confident expectation of what is ahead for the Christian. It is the daily reminder that this world is not our home and we must fix our gaze on eternity and on Jesus. This will be a huge theme throughout the book of Colossians as we are urged to set our minds not on the temporal things of this world, but on the things above (Colossians 3:2-4). And throughout this book we will be reminded that it is Jesus Himself who is our hope of glory (Colossians 1:27).

Our hope is Jesus. And it is on Him that we fix our gaze. And as we seek to live lives that demonstrate these marks of discipleship, we recognize that it is Jesus to whom we look toward. We look to Him as the example of perfect faith, love, and hope. And we look to Him for the strength to help us to walk in His ways. Because the call to discipleship is the call to be like Jesus.

Our hope is Jesus.

How is faith demonstrated in Jesus and in the life of the believer?

_____

_____

_____

_____

_____

_____

_____

How is love demonstrated in Jesus and in the life of the believer?

_____

_____

_____

_____

_____

_____

_____

How is hope demonstrated in the life of the believer?

_____

_____

_____

_____

_____

_____

_____

Our hope is rooted in the gospel.

THE FRUIT OF THE GOSPEL

Colossians 1:5–8

———

As Paul speaks of the hope that is laid up in heaven for believers, he shifts his focus to the gospel. It is the gospel that is the focus of the verses in today's passage. Paul reminds us that the hope that we have is a result of the gospel. Our hope is rooted in the gospel. The gospel is truth and comfort for our weary hearts. The gospel is the truth and the truth is the gospel. And just as Paul showed that faith and love are rooted in hope, he shows us that faith, love, and hope are all rooted in the gospel. The gospel is the word of truth. It is the message of the Bible and the plan of redemption. The gospel is the message of Jesus who came to save sinners. It is the message of justification, sanctification, and glorification. We cling to the gospel with everything that we are and stake our lives on its timeless truth.

Paul personifies the gospel as one that has come near to us. It is a beautiful picture of God drawing near to us, and a testament to the miracle of the incarnation, that God Himself became a man to be our Immanuel. He came to be God with us. It is a reminder of the initiating love of God that seeks out sinners with the message of the gospel that sets captives free and gives sight to the blind. God has pursued us — He has come to us when we had no power to come to Him. Jesus has come to live the life that we could not live and die the death that we deserved. He has come to atone for the sins of His people. He has come to bring abundant life that is only found in Him. He has come.

The gospel goes forth to the entire world. It goes out to all people groups. As Paul wrote these words, there were those who thought that Jesus was the Savior of the Jews only, but Paul puts a striking emphasis on the truth that the message of the gospel goes forth from God to all nations as God calls out His people from every people group of the entire world.

———

This gospel is bearing fruit. It is bearing fruit around the world as it goes out and multiplies. The language here calls to mind the command of Genesis for Adam and Eve to be fruitful and multiply (Genesis 1:28). It calls our minds back to the promise that God would raise up a people for Himself found in the Abrahamic Covenant (Genesis 12:1-3). And now here we see that the gospel itself is bearing fruit and increasing around the entire world.

The gospel has pursued us, and it is the gospel that grows us. The gospel is not just for the moment of salvation, but for every moment of the life of the Christian as well. Paul does not simply look to the work that the gospel is doing around the world as sinners are converted. He also looks to the immediate context of the believers in Colossae. The gospel grows and transforms us as the people of God. Little by little and from one degree of glory to the next, we are being transformed into the image of Christ (2 Corinthians 3:18). The gospel is bearing fruit. And as Jesus reminded us in John 15, we bear fruit only as we abide in Him. From the day that we heard and understood the message of the gospel to this very moment, God is working in our hearts and helping us to see His overflowing grace.

But the gospel must be learned. There is no such thing as someone who has been a Christian all of their life. In order for us to respond to God's initiating love and grace, we must hear the truth of the gospel of Jesus' perfect life, death, and resurrection. We must see the depths of our sin and be transformed by the grace of God. And we must first learn this message. As we see here and in other passages such as Romans 10:14-17, God's chosen method is through the proclamation of God's Word. We cannot be converted without the hearing of the gospel message. Paul here points us to Epaphras as a faithful teacher of God's Word who had shared the gospel with those at Colossae.

The message of the gospel points us to Jesus and it is through abiding in Him that we are transformed day by day. We need the gospel every single day. We need to be reminded of our own sin and weakness and of God's abundant strength. We take the gospel to our neighbors and to the ends of the earth with the confidence that it will bear fruit because it is the power of God (Romans 1:16). We sit under faithful preaching and we teach the Bible to others because God has revealed Himself in His Word. We trust that little by little God is making us a new creation. He is multiplying His people and building His Kingdom. He is bearing fruit in our hearts as we cling to the hope of the gospel.

It is the gospel that grows us.

Verse 6 says that the gospel has come to us. How did the gospel come to you?

_____

_____

_____

_____

Wherever the gospel goes, it bears fruit. How does that impact the way you think, act, and pray about what is happening in your own life and around the world?

_____

_____

_____

_____

_____

What does this passage teach you about the need for biblical teaching and preaching?

_____

_____

_____

_____

How does the gospel change the way we live our everyday lives?

_____

_____

_____

_____

_____

THE
PERSEVERANCE
OF THE SAINTS IS
MADE POSSIBLE
BY THE
PRESERVING HAND
OF THE LORD.

WALK WORTHY

Colossians 1:9-10

———

In these verses, Paul transitions from his thanksgiving to his prayer for the Colossian church. The words of Paul that are found here teach us how we should pray for our fellow believers, and also instruct us in how we should live as believers. Paul's words are intensely practical for our lives and transformative for our thoughts. We are being called to go deeper and to live lives that overflow with praise and faithfulness to the One who has been faithful to us.

The thanksgiving and prayer sections at the start of Colossians have many similarities and parallel statements. Paul is praying that the Colossians will continue through the power of the Spirit in the way of Christ and the path of sanctification. He prays for their perseverance and steadfastness in the faith. This is essential as they stand against false teachers who seek to present to them a false gospel, or to mix the wisdom of the world with the wisdom of God. He desires for them to stand firm, knowing that God will enable them to do so. The perseverance of the saints is made possible by the preserving hand of the Lord.

He asks that they would be filled with the knowledge of the will of God. This is the message of Scripture, and the eternal plan of God. The will of God is found in the Word of God, and Paul prays that the church would be filled with the knowledge of His will and His Word. In these two verses, we see a progression of growth that takes place after the gospel has taken root. Central to this growth process is the living and active Word of God. It is on the pages of God's Word that His will is revealed.

The knowledge of the will of God and the Word of God should be demonstrated in spiritual wisdom and understanding. We do not seek after knowledge for knowledges' sake. We do not come to the Bible to be able to spew out facts, but for spiritual wisdom and understanding. God's Word grows us little by little. And knowledge should compel us to action. As Paul continues in verse ten, we see that he prays that this knowledge, wisdom, and understanding will lead believers to walk in a manner worthy of the Lord. The Christian life is one of transformation. As we come to God's Word, we are to be compelled to action and transformation through the power of the Spirit in us.

We are to walk worthy of the Lord. This is made possible only through the work of Christ in us. There is nothing worthy that is in us apart from Christ in us. Yet through His power and His overwhelming grace, we can be changed from the way that we once were. As we grow in godliness and Christlikeness, we bear fruit. We were created for good works (Ephesians 2:10). We see here again an illusion to the creation narrative in Genesis. God's people are His new creation, and they are multiplying and bearing fruit because of His sovereign work of creation. We are not saved by our good works, but we are saved for good works. There is nothing that we can do to earn salvation, or God's love and favor, but as believers we are commanded to pursue holiness. That pursuit of holiness is the natural outpouring of our pursuit of the God who has pursued us first.

As we walk worthy and bear fruit, we increase in the knowledge of God. Here we see the cyclical pattern of the passage. As we grow in our knowledge of the will and Word of God, it is demonstrated in spiritual wisdom and understanding, and in holy living. And as we live lives of holiness that are immersed in the Word of God, we begin to know God more. This is the pattern of the Christian life that should be continually repeated—knowing His Word, living for His glory, and knowing God more.

Jesus has walked the road before us, and it is through our union with Him that this pattern of the Christian life is made possible. Growth, transformation, and holiness are not possible in our own strength. And the Christian life cannot be lived in our own strength, but in His. The call for us is to abide in Christ, cling to Him, and bear fruit for His glory.

As we come to God's Word, we are to be compelled to action and transformation through the power of the Spirit in us.

These verses are part of Paul's prayer list for the Colossian church. List out below the things from these verses that Paul was praying for them:

_____

_____

_____

_____

What do these requests teach you about how you should pray for others?

_____

_____

_____

_____

What do these requests teach you about how you should live?

_____

_____

_____

_____

Read John 15:1-17. How does this passage help you understand what it means to abide and bear fruit?

_____

_____

_____

_____

_____

COLOSSIANS 3:12

*Therefore, as God's chosen ones,
holy and dearly loved, put on
compassion, kindness, humility,
gentleness, and patience*

WEEK ONE REFLECTION

Paraphrase the passage from this week.

_____
_____
_____
_____
_____
_____
_____
_____

What did you observe from this week's text about God and His character?

_____
_____
_____
_____
_____
_____
_____
_____

What does this passage teach about the condition of mankind and about yourself?

_____
_____
_____
_____
_____
_____
_____
_____

How does this passage point to the gospel?

_____
_____
_____
_____
_____
_____
_____
_____
_____

How should you respond to this passage? What is the personal application?

_____
_____
_____
_____
_____
_____
_____
_____
_____
_____

What specific action steps can you take this week to apply this passage?

_____
_____
_____
_____
_____
_____
_____
_____

THIS IS

WHAT WE

WERE

MADE FOR.

THE POWER OF HIS GLORY

Colossians 1:11

In thanksgiving and prayer, Paul prays for the Colossians to be filled with the knowledge of God and the knowledge of His sovereign will as it is revealed in His Word. Paul wants the church at Colossae and us today to know God. This is why we were created. This is what we were made for. And then Paul prayed for them to walk worthy of the Lord. He urges them, and us, to live lives that put the gospel on display and bring honor to our Savior. This manner of life is one that is rooted in the knowledge of God and of His Word. And now in verse 11, Paul prays for the power that makes walking worthy possible.

Paul knows that in our own strength these things are impossible, but Paul also knows that as believers, we are not called to live in our own strength. And here in this verse we find out that what God desires from us, He provides for us. God desires us to live holy lives, and He gives us the strength to do it. Paul's prayer for believers is that they would be strengthened with all power, and this power Paul tells us is according to the glorious might of God. It is the glory of our God that enables us to live for His glory.

What is this power that Paul speaks of? He has spoken of this glorious power in many of his letters. In Romans 1:16, he reminded us that the gospel itself is the power of God for salvation. The gospel has power to transform us in salvation, and to moment by moment transform us into His image. In Ephesians 1:19-20, Paul points out that the power that is at work in us as believers is the same power that raised Jesus from the dead. This is the power that is inside us. The power and the glory of God that raised Jesus from the dead are at work in the people of God, and they are enabling us to walk in newness of life (Romans 6:4).

We are strengthened by His glory and the power of the gospel. But why? The second half of the verse continues, but it may not be the answer that we were expecting. Paul tells us that we are strengthened for endurance and patience with joy. The power of God in us does not mean that suffering will never come. The power of God in us means that God is with us when suffering comes. The power that raised Jesus from the dead and raised us from death to new life also empowers us to endure suffering with patience and joy.

The Christian life is not a life free from suffering, but the suffering that comes is never a surprise to God. Jesus has walked the road before us, and now through our union with Him, we carry on in His strength and not our own. Christians can face the sorrow of this world with joy in their hearts because they know the end of the story. Paul himself beautifully displayed this in his own life as he sang to God is prison (Acts 16:25), and as he ministered from the bondage of his chains. Our song is not dependent on our situation. Our song is dependent on our Savior. And Jesus never fails.

The joy of the Christian is a mystery to the world that points to the hope of the gospel. Endurance and patience are extremely similar, and yet theologians note that endurance most often refers to circumstances, and patience most often refers to our relationships with people. Our circumstances may bring us sorrow, and people may bring hurt and suffering, but God calls us to endure with patience the road that He has set before us.

At the end of the verse is a word that we do not often associate with endurance or patience. Our response to sorrow and suffering, and the way that we endure and are patient, is *joyfully*. We walk with joy even when the road is difficult, and the path is dark. We walk with joy because we know that Jesus has walked the long and treacherous road before us, and now He is in us and we are in Him. Through union with Christ, we walk ahead into the unknown with confidence. He has never failed us, and He never will. We will walk in joy because we have Jesus.

We carry on in His strength and not our own.

Read Romans 1:16. What does this verse tell us is the power of God?

_____

_____

_____

_____

_____

_____

How do we receive the power and strength of which Paul wrote?
Is this something that happens once or continually?

_____

_____

_____

_____

_____

_____

Read James 1:2-4. How do these verses help you to understand how believers should respond to suffering and trials?

_____

_____

_____

_____

_____

_____

_____

We should be thankful people.

GIVING THANKS FOR WHAT HE HAS DONE

Colossians 1:12-14

———

In verse 11, Paul spoke of being strengthened by the power of God for the purpose of living lives characterized by endurance, patience, and joy. Now he continues and speaks of another marker that should be present in the lives of God's people. We should be thankful people. Our lives should abound with thanksgiving to God for what He alone has done. Our salvation has been accomplished by His gracious hand, and we rejoice and give thanks for what He has done.

It nearly seems that Paul uses bullet points to remind us of what God has done and what it is that we should be giving thanks for. By doing so, Paul reminds us of the gospel and turns our hearts to remember the goodness of God in the lives of His people. The first thing that God has done is to qualify us to share in the inheritance of the saints. The language is reminiscent of the Old Testament language of Israel's inheritance of the promised land. The word Saints speaks of the chosen and set apart people of God. Paul is showing us in this passage the expansion of our understanding of both the inheritance of God's people and of God's people themselves. The inheritance of God's people is no longer a small strip of land in the Middle East; it is Christ Himself, and will one day be the entire earth in the new creation. And the people of God are no longer the people of a geographical Israel, but of a spiritual Israel made up of the people of God from every tribe, tongue, and nation (Ephesians 2:11-22, Galatians 3:7-9, 28-29). We have been qualified because we are in Jesus. Through the initiating love of the Father, the redemption found in the Son, and the work of the Spirit, we are brought near to God.

———

He has not only qualified us, but He has also delivered us and transferred us. Just as Israel was delivered out of Egypt, we have been delivered out of our sin. Our citizenship has been transferred and this world is no longer our home. We belong to the kingdom of God. Just as Moses delivered the people of Israel out of the bondage of Egypt, Jesus has delivered us out of the bondage of our sin. He has delivered us out of the darkness and depravity that we once walked in, and He has transferred us into His own kingdom. He has done it. Our deliverance is not dependent on anything that we have done or could possibly do, but it is dependent on what He has done.

Verse 14 ends this section by telling us that it is in Him that we have redemption and forgivingness. The verse has a striking parallel to Ephesians 1:7. Our redemption is found by Him, through Him, and in Him. And there is no other way of redemption and forgiveness. Our sins are washed clean by the blood of the Lamb, and our hearts are transformed by His grace. Paul closes this opening section by again reminding the church at Colossae that this is all made possible due to their position and spiritual location. They are in Christ, and it is in Him that their redemption is found; He enables them to walk in a worthy manner. It is in Him that they can endure with patience, joy, and thanksgiving the path that He has set before them.

Just as it is God who had accomplished their redemption, it is God who will keep them. As Paul urges them to walk in holiness, He also reminds them of their position of holiness before God. Because of the gospel, they are secure. The God who has saved them will not leave them, but will walk with them through each moment of this life until they see His face. Paul wanted them to know who they were in Him. No circumstance of life could shake that identity, no false teaching would change that position, and not even their own sin and struggles could change that reality. They were Christ's and He was holding them fast.

This is good news for us who are the people of God. God has done the work of our salvation, and He will preserve us and allow us to persevere in His grace. The timeless truths of the gospel are the anchor that remind us to continue in His love. The gospel reorients our minds and changes our hearts at the moment of our salvation, and also every day of the journey.

————

We have been qualified because we are in Jesus.

According to today's passage, what are the things that God has done for His people?

_____

_____

_____

_____

_____

_____

How do these verses shape the way we think about our identity?

_____

_____

_____

_____

_____

_____

How does remembering what God has done enable us to walk in His grace?

_____

_____

_____

_____

_____

_____

REST IN THE
SUFFICIENCY
OF JESUS CHRIST
OUR SAVIOR.

THE SUPREMACY AND SUFFICIENCY OF CHRIST

Colossians 1:15–17

———

Paul closes his thanksgiving and prayer with mention of Jesus, the beloved Son. And it seems that as we read, the mention of the person of Jesus thrusts Paul into worship and adoration. This portion of Scripture is often referred to as a hymn. Though we can't be sure if it was a hymn sung in the early church, its poetic qualities are clear. Line after line provides a compelling picture of the risen Christ.

The words of this passage highlight for us the supremacy and sufficiency of Jesus. Paul uses vivid descriptions to proclaim that Jesus is supreme and to be worshiped. And yet, He also compels us to rest in the sufficiency of Jesus Christ our Savior. Jesus is everything and Jesus is all that we need.

Verse 15 begins by declaring that Jesus is the image of the invisible God. Jesus is God made visible. He is fully God, while also being fully man. And if we want to know who God is, we must look to Jesus because it is through Jesus that God is revealed to us. In Christ we see a God who has created all things, who reigns over all things, and yet has come near to us. Through the miracle of the incarnation, God became a man and entered into our humanity. In Jesus, we behold the radical love of God that breaks down barriers and pursues us in love. Through Jesus, the glory of God that has always been invisible, has been gloriously made visible before our eyes.

He is the firstborn of all creation. Though He has always been, and the next verse will show us that He is the Creator, He is also the heir of creation. As the first-born son was the promised heir, Jesus is the heir of all the universe. Verse 16 continues by telling us that it is by Him that all things were created. From the spiritual powers to the powers of this world, all things were made by Him, all things were made through Him, and all things were made for Him. Every part of this world is for His glory.

Verse 17 tells us that He is before all things. Both in timing, as the one who is from the beginning, and in rank as the one who is above all things. And it is in Him that this world holds together. Our world is not held together by the force of nature, it is held together by the sovereign hand of the Son of God. We cannot take a single breath without Him. He is truly supreme and sufficient for us.

Over and over throughout the passage we see repetition used to point us to the majesty and beauty of Jesus. The passage is grounded by the phrase "He is." Paul grasps for words to describe God. And as we ourselves grasp at words to describe Him, we are reminded that He is everything. We worship because of who He is, and yet our words can never fully display the beauty of our God. His supremacy is demonstrated by Paul's use of the word all throughout the passage. He is our King and He is our Savior, and He is sovereign over all things. The multitude of prepositions remind us that everything in all of creation is by Him, through Him, for Him, and in Him. He is supreme and sufficient.

Paul gives us a picture of Jesus that calls us to worship. His majesty, dominion, and beauty are on display. Yet, we must not lose sight of the truth that this transcendent God is also our Savior. Through the work of Jesus on the cross, the people of God are brought into relationship with Him. Through union with Christ, we are in Him and He is in us. He is glorious and majestic, and yet He is near to us. This truth must change the way we go about our days. This truth must anchor our hearts in the hope of salvation. This truth must lead our hearts to worship.

We cannot take a single breath without Him. He is truly supreme and sufficient for us.

How does this passage display the supremacy and sufficiency of Jesus?

_____

_____

_____

_____

_____

_____

_____

God is majestic and glorious, as well as personal and near to us.
Why is it important that we recognize both aspects of His character?

_____

_____

_____

_____

_____

_____

_____

How should the truth of who Jesus is change our daily lives?

_____

_____

_____

_____

_____

_____

Salvation is found only in Jesus.

THE PREEMINENT CHRIST

Colossians 1:18

———

Paul continues to point us to who Jesus is as he piles on descriptors of who Christ is in the midst of this beautiful hymn. While using the most beautiful words, we get the impression that Paul can't find enough words to describe the majesty, beauty, and glory of Jesus. Again, in this verse, we are being reminded of the supremacy and sufficiency of the Son of God. As the Colossian church struggled with false teachings that tried to convince them that their worship should include Jesus plus some other thing, Paul reminds them that all they need is Jesus. Jesus plus nothing is the message of gospel-hope that is found in this beautiful hymn, in the book of Colossians, and throughout the entire Bible. Salvation is found only in Jesus.

Paul tells us that Jesus is the head of the body, which is the church. The magnitude of this statement should not be overlooked. It is here that we see a shift in the hymn from a description of creation, to a description of a new creation. Paul points to the church as the new people of God. The church is the people called out and united to Christ. The illustration that Paul provides is one of a body where the church is the body and Christ is the head. This illustration shines a light on our utter dependence on Jesus. Just as the body cannot function without its head, we cannot function without our Savior. The illustration also speaks of our union with Christ. We are in Him, and He is in us. There is nothing that can separate us, we are one.

The illustration points us to the universal truth but holds great implications for local bodies of believers. As churches, we must keep Jesus at the center. Everything we do as a church should be centered on who He is and all that He has done, while seeking to bring Him glory through every part of everything that we do. In our worship, our preaching, our programs, and our communities, we must be distinctly Christ-centered.

———

As the verse continues, we see Jesus named as "the beginning." He is the source of all the world and the ruler of it. This phrase reminds us, just as earlier verses in the hymn did, that He is the Creator and the one who rules creation. And just as He is the beginning and source of our physical creation, He is also the beginning and source of our new creation.

In verse 15, Jesus was named as the firstborn of all creation, and here in verse 18, He is named as the firstborn from the dead. Just as Jesus is the one from which all creation originated from, so is He the one from which our resurrection is founded. His resurrection has guaranteed the spiritual resurrection of His people. Through our union with Him we were crucified with Christ and united with Him in His death. And in and through His resurrection, we are also raised to walk in newness of life (Romans 6:1-11). In salvation we already experience the resurrection of our inner man, and in eternity we will experience final resurrection. As He has been raised, we will also be raised.

The verse ends with the reminder that because of who He is and because of all that He is done, Jesus is preeminent. He is supreme over everything. This beautiful passage of Scripture portrays for us the cosmological nature of Jesus. He is supreme over the cosmos, and yet He also bends low to us. Supreme over all of creation, and yet so near to His people that it is in Him that we live and move and have our being (Acts 17:28). The all-sufficient Christ is all-sufficient for us.

His resurrection has guaranteed the spiritual resurrection of His people.

What does this verse tell us about Jesus? Who is He?

_____

_____

_____

_____

_____

_____

How do these aspects of who Jesus is impact our daily lives?

_____

_____

_____

_____

_____

_____

Look up the word preeminent and write its definition below:

_____

_____

_____

_____

_____

_____

THE CREATOR
OF ALL THINGS
BECAME LIKE THOSE
HE HAD CREATED
IN ORDER TO
RANSOM HIS OWN.

THE FULLNESS OF GOD

Colossians 1:19-20

In these final verses of the Christ hymn, we are once again compelled to worship Jesus our Savior for who He is and all that He has done for His people. Verse 19 shines a light on the overwhelming beauty of who Jesus is and the miracle of the incarnation. Verse 20 gives us just a glimpse of the magnitude of all that Jesus' atoning sacrifice has accomplished for His people. Along with the previous verses in the passage, we are given a picture of the majesty of our Savior, the gift of redemption, and our eternal hope.

Verse 18 showed us the preeminence and supremacy of Jesus, and as we move into verse 19, we are given a description of just why it is that Christ is preeminent over all things. It is here that we are told that it is in Him that all the fullness of God dwells. This is a statement of the absolute deity of Jesus. He is fully God and He is everything that God is. The full sum of God's attributes is within the person of Jesus Christ. God the Son has taken on flesh and come near to His people. Through the miracle of the incarnation, God Himself became a man. He felt the cool night air and the dust gathered on His feet on the roads of Galilee. He felt pain and emotions; and He faced every temptation that we have faced without ever sinning.

The apostle John told us that the Word became flesh and dwelt among us (John 1:14). The Creator of all things became like those that He had created in order to ransom His own. In the face of Jesus, we see the glory of God Himself. The language found in Colossians, John 1, and in many other places in Scripture is the language of dwelling. It is language that hearkens back to the Old Testament tabernacle or temple where God gave a picture of what Jesus would be. God Himself would draw near to His people, He would dwell among them, and literally pitch His tent in their midst. Paul has gone to great lengths in this beautiful hymn to show us the majesty, superiority, and supremacy of Jesus, and now He reminds us of the glorious truth that Jesus who is God incarnate has come near to us.

In verse 20, Paul declares that it is through Him that all things are reconciled to Him. These words remind us that in a fallen world that has been tainted by sin, reconciliation is needed. And the only answer to our desperate search for reconciliation and peace is found on a bloody cross outside the city limits of Jerusalem. The blood of His cross points us to His substitutionary atoning sacrifice. He has paid for the sins of His people. He has reconciled us to God. He has made peace.

The reconciliation of all things to Him is that all things will be rightly aligned under His sovereign rule. Paul reminds us that this renewal will take place on earth and in heaven. Paul uses cosmic language to show us the far reach of Christ's redemptive work. Scripture does not teach us here that all people will be saved or that things can be saved. Instead He points us to the magnitude of restoration. Even the creation groans for the return of Jesus and the consummation of a new heaven and new earth (Romans 8:18-25). There will be a day when all is made right, when justice will reign, and sin and evil will be no more.

Paul rightly speaks of these events as something that has already happened. We are reminded of the assurance that what God has already done, He will bring to completion. He has conquered all things, and He will make all things new. The price was paid at the cross and we await the day that we will see the full effect of what He has done. This is the already but not yet of our faith. As believers we experience a glimpse of that final restoration as our hearts are restored to God and there is peace between us and God. And yet with joy, we await the day when all things are restored to God's good design and sin and sorrow will be forever gone.

These vibrant truths should compel us to worship our Savior, and they should also urge us to live in light of eternity. We live with our hearts awakened to the truth that it is in Christ that these things are made possible, and with the joy in knowing that if we are His children, we are in Christ as well. We share the truth of God's reconciling and peace-making love with confidence, knowing that God has already accomplished the salvation of His people and He will draw them to Himself. We trust that though we see a world around us that has been broken and marred by sin, there will be a day when sin and death will be no more. The same Jesus who came near in a stable on that first Christmas will come again for His people.

What do these verses teach us about who Jesus is and what He has done?

_____

_____

_____

_____

_____

_____

What does the need for reconciliation teach us about the condition of humanity?

_____

_____

_____

_____

_____

_____

How does this passage give us confidence about what is ahead for God's people?
How does it help us to trust Him right now?

_____

_____

_____

_____

_____

_____

_____

_____

COLOSSIANS 3:13

bearing with one another and forgiving one another if anyone has a grievance against another. Just as the Lord has forgiven you, so you are also to forgive.

WEEK TWO REFLECTION

Paraphrase the passage from this week.

_____
_____
_____
_____
_____
_____
_____

What did you observe from this week's text about God and His character?

_____
_____
_____
_____
_____
_____
_____
_____

What does this passage teach about the condition of mankind and about yourself?

_____
_____
_____
_____
_____
_____
_____

How does this passage point to the gospel?

_____
_____
_____
_____
_____
_____
_____
_____

How should you respond to this passage? What is the personal application?

_____
_____
_____
_____
_____
_____
_____
_____

What specific action steps can you take this week to apply this passage?

_____
_____
_____
_____
_____
_____
_____

WE WERE
FAR FROM GOD
AND *HOPELESS*
ON OUR OWN.

YOU ARE NO LONGER WHO YOU ONCE WERE

Colossians 1:21-23

———

In these three verses, Paul presents for the Colossians and for believers, who they once were, what Christ has done, and how we should live in light of our new identity. It is a short primer on the Christian life. From who we were before conversion to who we will be in eternity, Paul is giving us a picture of the life of the believer in miniature form.

We read these words in context of the beautiful Christ hymn. We have seen the majesty and glory of our Savior, and now Paul shifts to look at the people of God. Yet even his glimpse of God's people is overflowing with the surpassing work and worth of Jesus who is our living hope. Paul begins by looking to the past. He speaks of who believers once were. This description is true for the Colossian believers, and it is true for every believer of all time. Before our redemption, this is the picture of us. We were alienated from God. We were hostile towards God. We were evil doers. We were alienated and separated from God by our sin. Yet, not only were we separated, but we were hostile toward God. We wanted to do things our own way. We wanted to live in our own strength. Our lives overflowed with sin and evil deeds. This is a picture of the total depravity of man after the fall. Sin had infected every part of us. We were far from God and hopeless on our own.

But there is hope, and verse 22 overflows with that hope. Paul follows a familiar structure that is often found in his writing. He contrasts what we once were, and then shows us what we now are in Christ. He shows us what we now are by showing us what Christ has done. We have already been shown who Jesus is and now we are reminded again of His work for us as His people. Though we saw the cosmic scope of the reconciling work of Christ in verse 20, here we see that this cosmic work reaches down into the hearts of God's people. He reconciles us to Himself through the cross.

Those who were once alienated from God, hostile toward God, and living lives of sin, have been transformed by God's grace and His work of redemption on the cross. Through His grace, we are reconciled to God and given the righteousness of Christ for our justification. Because we are in Christ and bear His righteousness, we are declared to be positionally holy and blameless before God. Through our journey as believers, we will still struggle with sin and fight against our flesh, but we are declared by God to be righteous at the moment of salvation. Through our entire lives and the process of sanctification, God is conforming us little by little into His image. And someday in eternity, we will stand before Him with our sanctification complete and sin removed. We live in hope that the little by little progress of holiness will be completed by God in the end.

Verse 23 teaches us how to live in the meantime. We preserve as the saints. We live for God's glory and continue in the faith. We root our hope in the living and abiding Word of God and walk steadfastly through the power of the Spirit in us. We persevere because it is God that does the work of preserving us through this life of testing and trials, sorrow and suffering. We live in light of who God has made us to be, not of any power of our own, but in His strength. We cling to the gospel that has been proclaimed throughout all parts of the world. We hold fast to the gospel that bears fruit wherever it goes and bears fruit in us (Colossians 1:6). We, like Paul, and the millions before us, give our lives to this gospel.

Through His grace, we are reconciled to God and given the righteousness of Christ for our justification.

What do these verses teach us about humanity and the fallen condition of man?

_____

_____

_____

_____

_____

_____

What does the passage teach us about the character of God?

_____

_____

_____

_____

_____

_____

How does God's character and action compel us to live?

_____

_____

_____

_____

_____

_____

All things are under the sovereign care
and control of our God.

TO MAKE THE WORD OF GOD FULLY KNOWN

Colossians 1:24-25

Paul's theological introduction to the letter of Colossians extolled the greatness and glory of Christ. For several verses, Paul shifts the focus to a very personal and heartfelt description of his own ministry and his desire for the young church of Colossae. Even in his description of his ministry, we are encouraged and exhorted to follow the Lord and to spread the message of the gospel which has the power to transform hearts and mature believers into what God has created them to be.

The description of Paul's ministry begins with a statement from Paul that he rejoices in his sufferings. This language sounds backward to us and perhaps out of place, but it is not out of place among the biblical authors. This is a theme that we see throughout the New Testament from Paul and other writers. In a time of immense pressure and persecution for Paul, he can declare that he is rejoicing in his sufferings. He does not rejoice in spite his sufferings, but he rejoices in them. Paul wisely understands that all things are under the sovereign care and control of our God. There is nothing that can stand against the will of our God. And though it doesn't make the trials disappear, Paul can face them with confidence in a sovereign God who is never caught off guard even when we are. In fact, Paul can face trials and sufferings with joy because he knows that though he doesn't understand how, God is working these trials for His glory and for the good of the people of God.

Paul is willing to face whatever trials may come for the people of God and the name of God. Though a part of the calling of every child of God, we are specifically told in the account of Paul's conversion that he would suffer for the name of Christ (Acts 9:16). These verses are not teaching that anything can be added to the finished work of Christ. This is clear to us from the full account of Scripture and from Paul's letter to the Colossians, but Paul is showing us that as believers we are called to live in light of our union with Christ. We are called to share in the sufferings of Christ and to walk in His footsteps of obedience and suffering. And yet we know that as we are united to Him in His suffering, we will also be united to Him in glory (Philippians 3:10, 2 Corinthians 1:5-6, 4:10-12). He is in us and we are in Him and we should live every day in light of that reality.

Paul identifies himself as a minister of God by the commission or stewardship that God had given him. He was uniquely called and equipped to do what God had called him to do. In the same way, each child of God has been uniquely gifted and sent to glorify God and to make disciples. In the rest of verse 25, and in the following verses, we will see that discipleship is Paul's focus. His goal is to share the Word and to allow it to bring the people of God to maturity.

The people of God are shaped by the Word of God. The Word of God is what God uses to grow His people into maturity. It is the means by which God speaks to His people and the instrument that He uses to sanctify them. It should be no mystery to us then why Paul speaks first and foremost about his desire to make the word of God fully known among the people of God. There is no greater means of growing in grace than through the living and abiding Word of God. Every ministry of our churches and every plan of discipleship must be rooted on this solid foundation. The Word of God is what forms us into the people that God has made us to be.

The pattern of discipleship and growing in grace must always begin with the Word of God. We must allow this truth to sink deep into our own hearts for the ministries we serve in and for our own hearts. If we want to grow in grace, we must grow in our knowledge of the Word. Albert Mohler has said, "Our spiritual maturity will never exceed our knowledge of the Bible." Though knowledge of the Bible does not equal spiritual maturity, you cannot be spiritually mature without knowledge of the Bible. May this truth spur us on to know God's Word fully. And through knowing the Word of God, may we know God more and be able to share who He is with those we meet.

The people of God are shaped by the Word of God.

What do you think the difference is between rejoicing in our sufferings and rejoicing in spite of them?

_____

_____

_____

_____

_____

_____

How can you rejoice in your sufferings right now?

_____

_____

_____

_____

_____

_____

Why is the Word of God so important for our growth as believers?

_____

_____

_____

_____

_____

_____

_____

THE PLAN

OF GOD *IS*

ETERNAL

CHRIST IN YOU, THE HOPE OF GLORY

Colossians 1:26-29

———

Paul has given us a clear picture of his mission to make the Word of God fully known among the Colossians and among all of the people of God. In this passage we continue to uncover insight into Paul's plan for discipleship and the mystery and center of the Christian faith.

Paul speaks of this great mystery that has been hidden for ages and is now revealed to the people of God. He is not speaking of a mystery in the sense of something strange and unusual, but in the sense of something that has been hidden. We are being given a glimpse at the unfolding plan of God and the progressive nature by which revelation is received. The plan of God is eternal, and yet it is revealed to us little by little throughout Scripture.

Another aspect of the mystery that Paul speaks of here is the inclusion of the gentiles into the people of God. This understanding was new to many Jewish believers, though the Old Testament had often spoken of people of every tribe, tongue, and nation worshiping the God of Israel. Paul Himself also taught this truth richly in his epistles and particularly in Ephesians 2 and 3. The gospel goes forth to all kinds of people and the people of God come from every people group of the world.

Paul points to the central aspect of the mystery and the central aspect of our faith — Christ in us the hope of glory. This is the message that Paul preaches to the Colossian church as they struggled against false teaching, and it is the message that rings out for every age. The gospel is centered on Christ. This is the mystery that we stake our faith on. We have union with Christ. He is in us and we are in Him.

———

This is our hope and our assurance. The message of the gospel is a message of a high and holy God who has condescended to His people and come near to us. It is the message of the King of Glory who has taken on flesh and has gone to the cross to accomplish salvation for His own. The gospel is the message of Jesus. So we preach, and we teach, and we proclaim this message—the gospel of Jesus—who is above all things.

Yesterday we saw that Paul's plan of discipleship was to make the Word of God fully known. We were reminded that it is God's Word that shapes and transforms the people of God, and now we see the goal of that understanding of the Word of God. Paul's goal and desire is that the people of God that have been taught and have learned the Word of God would mature in Christ. The Word of God is taught not for mere regurgitation of facts, but for transformation of the heart. The Word of God and the Spirit of God bring the people of God to maturity. This is the goal of discipleship: that God's people may be complete and equipped for every good work (2 Timothy 3:16-17). This is God's desire for His people.

Paul was keenly aware that this mission of discipleship was work. In verse 29, he speaks of toil and struggle. He was using words that referenced athletic games and the struggle to run the race and win the prize. These metaphors are no strangers to Paul's writings. Yet, as he speaks of working and struggling, he also speaks of working with the energy and power that are worked in Him by Christ. Paul is teaching us the powerful truth that we work because He works. We work through the power of the Spirit that is working within us. We press on in faithfulness because He is faithful. We persevere because He is preserving us. Even our perseverance is a work of God. From beginning to end we depend on Him. From our salvation to our sanctification we rely on the power of Christ in us and rest in the assurance that as God's people, we are in Christ.

These truths have radical applications to our everyday lives. We are reminded that we study the Word of God, not to merely gain academic knowledge, but to grow in our knowledge of God. This knowledge coupled with the matchless power of the Spirit grows us into maturity. We press on no matter what life brings, but we do not do it in our own strength. We press on through the power of Christ in us. We press on knowing that though we are weak, He is strong in us. We press on knowing that little by little, we are being transformed into the image of Christ until the day we see His face.

In what ways was the gospel a mystery in the ages and generations past?

_____

_____

_____

_____

_____

Look up the word mature in a dictionary. What do you think it means to be mature in Christ?

_____

_____

_____

_____

How does a person mature in Christ?

_____

_____

_____

_____

Verse 29 reminds us that we work because God is working in and through us.
How does this give you hope for the situations you are facing in life right now?

_____

_____

_____

_____

_____

Our salvation is accomplished in God alone.

JESUS IS ALL THAT WE NEED

Colossians 2:1-5

Jesus is all that we need. This is the message that Paul brings before us. Though false teachers had crept into the church and tried to make the Colossians question the truth of the statement that Jesus is all that the people of God needed, Paul fervently points the Colossians back to the truth that our salvation is accomplished in God alone. There is no other thing, no other philosophy, no other earthly wisdom that is needed. We need Christ alone.

Though beginning a new section, Paul continues on by conveying the message of his struggle for the Colossians. He desires for the people of Colossae and the people of Laodicea just a few miles away to be firmly rooted in the truth of the Word of God. He wanted them to grow to maturity. Though he couldn't see them face to face, he pleads with them through this letter to cling to the truth, and ultimately to cling to Jesus.

Paul desires for the people to be encouraged by the Word of God. We are pointed to a cycle of the Christian life that we must be reminded of. The people of God are knit together in love as they learn the Word of God together and grow in their knowledge and understanding of who God is. And as we grow in our knowledge and understanding of the Word and character of God, we will be continually knit together with the community of believers. As we go deeper in the Word and grow deeper in gospel application, we continue to grow deeper in community that stirs our affections for Christ. This should be a normative cycle in the life of the believer.

Throughout the book of Colossians, we will continually be pointed to Christ, and this passage is no different. The knowledge of God's mystery is Jesus. Paul spent the majority of the first chapter pointing us to rich Christology and now he is again pointing us to the centrality and sufficiency of our risen Savior.

As we are pointing to Christ and being reminded of His all-sufficiency, we are reminded that Jesus is all that we need. He is all that we need because it is in Him that all wisdom and knowledge reside. With false teachers threatening the Colossian church with a message of Jesus plus philosophy and earthly wisdom, Paul boldly stands for the truth that the message of the gospel is Jesus plus nothing. We have no need to run after the world's wisdom when we have been given the wisdom of God in His Word. We have no need to chase after the next best thing or the newest philosophy. As believers, we have union with Christ. He is in us and we are in Him. All wisdom and knowledge are in Him, and we are in Him.

Paul doesn't hide his motivation for the poignant words that he writes. He wants the Colossian believers, and all believers, to be equipped to stand for truth in the midst of a world of lies. The message of the world and their philosophy may even seem plausible and compelling, but our standard of truth is not our emotions or plausible arguments. Our standard of truth is the unchanging and enduring Word of God. He is teaching them the richness of who Christ is so that they will not be deceived by the counterfeit religions of the world. The world's promises of hope are empty promises because hope and peace are found only in Jesus. He is the only one who satisfies.

The message of Christ is a message that is just as applicable to us today as it was to the Colossian church. Truth is not hidden from us as the people of God. It has been revealed to us through the person of Jesus. For every struggle and every disappointment, He is what we need. The world will try to give us an answer to what we need to find peace, hope, and happiness. But the things that the world provides will never satisfy our souls. Our souls were not made to be satisfied by the things of this world. Our souls were made to be satisfied by our God. So we can approach our daily lives and our deepest sufferings with hope and encouragement because we are in Christ and He is all that we need.

Our standard of truth is the unchanging and enduring Word of God.

Paul was passionate about the Colossians knowing Christ and the truth of God's Word. How can you demonstrate this care for others?

_____

_____

_____

In this passage we see a cycle that as God's people grow in the Word, they also grow in love for one another. Have you seen this to be true in your own life? In what areas of your life can you continue this cycle?

_____

_____

_____

_____

In this passage, we are reminded that Jesus is all that we need. What does the world communicate that people need? What are things that you sometimes think you need?

_____

_____

_____

_____

How does the message of the sufficiency of Christ change the way that we approach our daily lives?

_____

_____

_____

_____

OUR *ACTIONS*
SHOULD FLOW
FROM WHAT
GOD HAS
DONE FOR US.

ROOTED IN HIM

Colossians 2:6-7

—

These two verses distill for us the central message of the entire book of Colossians. We find here the reminder of the centrality of Christ, while also being told what our response should be. This passage is a beautiful mixture of the description of Christ found in the hymn of chapter one and the practical exhortation found later in the book. It is a timely reminder for us that our actions should flow from what God has done for us. We grow in Christ in the same way that we came to Christ—by His grace.

Verse six begins with therefore or so then. This serves to point our attention to the fact that what Paul is about to say is fully based on what he has already said. We read these words in light of the earlier words of Colossians. It should come as no surprise that the foundation that is pointed to is Christ. Paul has spent the entire letter pointing us to Jesus, and these verses are no different. Just as we have received Christ, we are to walk in Him. Jesus is the center of our lives as believers. We live from Him, for Him, and in Him.

The concept of receiving Christ that is being referenced here is the act of hearing, learning, and receiving the gospel message. It is not confined to praying a prayer as our culture would often think of receiving Christ, instead it is the entire process of God pursuing us in grace, the hearing of the message of the gospel, and receiving it by faith. It is first and foremost a work of God in drawing our hearts to Himself through the power of the gospel. The way we are to live is in the same way that we have received Him, through His grace. Paul reminds us that the One who we have received and the One who we are to walk in is Jesus Christ the Lord. It is the same Jesus who was poetically described for us in chapter one. It is by Him and through Him that the world was created, it is for Him that everything exists, and it is in Him that all things are held together. And this sovereign King is our Savior and Lord.

—

We are commanded to walk in Him. We do not walk in our own strength, but in His grace. We have been rescued by grace to walk in grace. Paul continues to explain our position and our response in verse seven. We are rooted and built up in Him. The word rooted here is in the Greek aorist tense. It denotes a once for all action. It reminds us that we have been united to Christ and rooted into Him through our conversion. Like a seed planted in the ground, we are called to grow and bear fruit. He is our root and from Him, through Him, and in Him we grow.

We are rooted deeply in Him, and yet also built up in Him. Here the metaphor changes from that of a tree or plant, to an architectural structure. We are built up in Him. The Greek tense here is the present tense and is designating a continual action. We are to be in a constant state of being built up in Him. This should be the normal and daily pattern of the Christian life. We are to be continually built up and established in Christ who is our Lord. We are to live in light of the gospel that we have received and the gospel that we have been taught. Gospel-centered teaching should lead to gospel trans-formation, and gospel-centered living.

Paul ends these verses with an exhortation of something that should be a hallmark of the Christian life. We should be a people of thanksgiving. Worship and thanksgiving should be our response to the rich theology that Paul is teaching us. Thanksgiving should overflow from our hearts, our lives, and our lips. When we see the supremacy of our Savior and the hope of the gospel, we must be led to worship. Our speech should over-flow with thankfulness for all that God has done. We should proclaim His goodness with every breath. His faithfulness should be always on our hearts.

This is what God has called us to. To be so intimately reminded of what God has done for us, to be continually growing in Him, and to be overflowing with thanksgiving no matter what our situation or our circumstance. We have all that we need, because we have Jesus and we need nothing else.

We have been rescued by grace to walk in grace.

How does verse 6 point us to the supremacy of Christ?

_____

_____

_____

What does it mean to walk in Him?

_____

_____

_____

_____

If you are a child of God, you are already rooted in Christ. How should this change the way that you think and live?

_____

_____

_____

The life of the Christian should be marked by thanksgiving and worship. Take a moment to record your thanksgiving for who God is and all that He has done for you.

_____

_____

_____

_____

_____

_____

COLOSSIANS 3:14

*Above all, put on love, which is
the perfect bond of unity.*

WEEK THREE REFLECTION

Paraphrase the passage from this week.

_____
_____
_____
_____
_____
_____
_____
_____

What did you observe from this week's text about God and His character?

_____
_____
_____
_____
_____
_____
_____
_____

What does this passage teach about the condition of mankind and about yourself?

_____
_____
_____
_____
_____
_____
_____

How does this passage point to the gospel?

How should you respond to this passage? What is the personal application?

What specific action steps can you take this week to apply this passage?

IN CHRIST

WE HAVE

ALL THAT

WE NEED.

IN HIM

Colossians 2:8-10

———

In Christ, we have all that we need. Though the world would seek to convince us that there is more that we need, Jesus is more than enough for us. As Paul writes to the church at Colossae, he wants them to understand this truth. And as we read these words 2000 years later, the timeless truths stand unchanged. Though the world has a list of things people need to be happy and successful, all that we need is Jesus.

Paul begins these verses with a command as he urges believers to not be taken captive by the mindset of this world. He breaks this down for us by pointing out many of the things that the world tries to convince us are necessary. As disciples of Christ, we must be aware of these false philosophies and ideologies, and through the power of Christ, cling to the truth of Christ. We must be disciples of Christ and not disciples of this world. The philosophy of the world, the empty deceit of false teachers and false gospels, the traditions of men, and the false gods of the world are presented to us as necessities, but Paul tells us that they are not.

These areas that easily take believers captive are very similar today. Though perhaps they are nuanced by slightly different types of philosophy and false teachings, the basis of the false teachings remains the same. Just as the Colossians were up against false teachers who told them that they needed something more, so are we. Anything that adds to the gospel is not the gospel. While the philosophies of the world call for believers to look to the world for hope and wisdom, disciples are called to look to Christ alone. It is in Him that all the treasures of knowledge and wisdom are found (Colossians 2:3). We must firmly plant our gaze on Jesus.

Paul presents us with a compelling case for fixing our eyes on Jesus and not being deceived and distracted by the ways of this world. By echoing the words of chapter one, our gaze is redirected from the wisdom of this world to Jesus where all wisdom dwells. We are reminded that it is in Christ that all the fullness of God dwells. This dwelling is bodily. It is not merely a hypothetical statement; it is a literal reality. In the body of our risen Savior is all the fullness and matchless character of our God. We have no need to run to the wisdom of this world when the wisdom of God dwells in our risen Savior.

Verse 10 gives us a grand crescendo that declares to us the reason why we can turn from the ways of this world and to Christ. In Christ, all the wisdom and fullness of God dwells, and we are in Him. We have been filled with Him and in Him. We have union with Christ as the people of God. We have all that we need in Jesus. And because of His Spirit in us, and our position in union with Him, though the world seeks to take us captive, we can take every thought captive to the obedience of Christ (2 Corinthians 10:5). Though not yet fully free from the presence of sin, we are free from sin's penalty and sin's power. And though at this present moment we find ourselves in this world that is not our home, we are also seated in the heavenly places with Christ (Ephesians 2:5-6). We are united to the all-sufficient Savior. We live in this world in light of the reality of our union with Christ and it should change the way that we live every moment.

What does this mean for our lives? Our union with Christ has practical applications for our daily lives. We must cling to Christ and be saturated in His Word so that we will not be easily swayed by the philosophy of this world. We must grow in grace as disciples who have been transformed and united to our Savior. We must grow in grace in community with believers that will challenge and encourage us to cling to Christ alone. We must change our thinking and take every thought captive. We must remember. We must remember what God has done and who He is and live in light of that truth, instead of the lies that this world has to offer. Day by day, and moment by moment we must cling to Jesus. He is all that we need.

In Christ, all the wisdom and fullness of God dwells, and we are in Him.

In these verses Paul gave several examples of things that take people captive.
What things have you observed that take people captive?

_____

_____

_____

_____

_____

_____

How does the picture of Jesus that Paul gives remind us that Jesus is all that we need?

_____

_____

_____

_____

_____

_____

In Jesus, we have all that we need. How can you live like this is true?

_____

_____

_____

_____

_____

_____

God did not leave His people

in their spiritual death.

UNITED TO HIM

Colossians 2:11-15

———

Throughout this section of the book of Colossians, Paul wants us to see the importance and overwhelming truth of believers' union with Christ. We are in Him and He is in us. In this passage, we see some of the implications of that union. The importance of this union cannot be overstated.

Paul first points us to circumcision. He tells us that as believers, we have been circumcised with an inward circumcision. This is a circumcision not of physical bodies, but of the hearts of God's people. The concept of an inward circumcision is not foreign to even the Old Testament. In passages such as Deuteronomy 30:6, we see that God's people were to have circumcised hearts. Paul reminds us that this inward circumcision is made possible only by Jesus and through faith in Him. It is through this inward transformation that the flesh is put off. Though believers will not experience freedom from sin's presence on this earth, through salvation believers are freed from the penalty and power of sin in their lives.

Paul then shifts our attention to baptism and our union with Christ. Baptism is a symbol of the new covenant, and it points to our union with Christ. Just as in baptism, believers were buried with Christ, and then raised to walk in newness of life in the Spirit. Baptism points to a spiritual reality of our union with Christ. And the power that has raised believers from spiritual death is the same power that raised Jesus from the dead. The work of the resurrection of Christ and of the resurrection of believers is a trinitarian resurrection. We are raised by the Father through the power of the Spirit because of the finished work of the Son.

Verse 13 speaks of the condition of sinners apart from Christ. We are dead in trespasses and sins. We are spiritually dead and far from God. Paul speaks also of the gentiles who are not only dead in their sin, but who are also uncircumcised and cut off from the covenant. The passage has very close parallels to Ephesians 2 where these same concepts are also explained. The desperation of our condition is displayed here in these verses. A dead person has no power to raise themselves and there is nothing that we could do to resurrect the hopelessness of our life apart from Christ. But God did not leave His people in their spiritual death, He made us alive. We are made alive in Christ.

Our spiritual resurrection has taken place because we are in Christ, and it is fully dependent on God and the work of Christ on the cross. There is nothing that we could do to earn this great salvation. The record of our debt has been canceled and the legal demands of the law have been fulfilled. What we could not do for ourselves, Christ did for us. And when Jesus was nailed to the cross, the crash of the hammer into the nails that pierced his hands and feet nailed the sins of God's people to the cross of Calvary. The debt was not excused; it was paid for. The precious blood of Christ has been shed that the people of God may be free. The powers of hell have been disarmed and the curse of sin has been removed. Jesus has overcome. This is the good news of the gospel.

He paid our debt. He set us free. He redeemed His own. There was nothing that we could do to earn this love, but Christ has poured out this grace on His own. We stand in awe of this truth. Now as the people of God, we are fully and completely united to Christ. When He died, we died with Him. When He was raised, we were raised to spiritual life with Him. Now we live in Him, through Him, and for Him. We are His. This should change our perspective on our every moment. We now live in the victory that has been made possible by our victorious King.

—

We are made alive in Christ.

What is union with Christ?

_____

_____

_____

_____

_____

_____

_____

Read Romans 6:3-11. What does this teach you about your union with Christ?
How should that union change the way that you live?

_____

_____

_____

_____

_____

_____

What does this passage teach you about God and His character?

_____

_____

_____

_____

_____

_____

WE HAVE
SOMETHING
MUCH BETTER THAN
A SHADOW AND
A PICTURE.

HOLDING FAST

Colossians 2:16-19

———

Paul begins today's passage with the word therefore and points the Colossians back to the truth of Christ's victory and our union with Him as he begins to shift topics. He wants the Colossians and us to be rooted in the truth of who Christ is and what He has accomplished along with the truth of our own identity as we think through the false teachings that were beginning to permeate the church at Colossae. We need the truth of who Christ is and who we are in Him to transform our thinking and every ounce of our being. Paul urges the church to not stray from the basic tenants of the gospel that provide the lens by which we must view every facet of life.

The Colossian people were up against false teachers who wanted Jesus plus all the additional things that they deemed necessary for salvation and fullness of life. In these verses it seems as though Paul is referencing many of the aspects of Judaism that some were trying to enforce on converts to Christ. From the keeping of kosher food laws to the festivals and holy days of the Old Testament, there were many preaching that in addition to faith in Christ, it was necessary for believers to participate in the ceremonial law. Paul clearly shows us in verse 17 that the ceremonial law was but a shadow of Christ. Now that Christ has come, we have something much better than a shadow and a picture. We have Christ Himself who is the substance that these symbols pointed toward.

All of the law and the rich ceremonial symbolism was fulfilled in Jesus. There was and is no need for believers to return to the rituals and symbols because Jesus is with His people. Every aspect of the law is fulfilled in Christ. The shadow was beautiful, but the substance is beyond comprehension. Jesus has come and we have no need for a mere shadow.

Paul also addresses the spiritual mysticism that was present in Colossae. In the same way as those who thought that the believers must have Jesus plus the keeping of the Jewish ceremonial law, there were many

———

who wanted to add secular mysticism to Christianity. Again, Paul's response is to beware of both the false teaching that is presented and those who do so in pride. He warns of those who do not cling to Christ and those who do not draw their strength from Him alone.

The warning of how these false teachers do not cling to Christ is an admonition to us to hold fast to Christ. We hold fast to Him because He is holding fast to us. We persevere because of His preserving hand upon us. Jesus is the head of the body, and it is from Him that all wisdom and insight, nourishment and growth are found. There is no philosophy that will heal our souls, only Jesus can.

Paul uses the illustration of the body to remind us that our growth comes from Jesus who is our head. We cling to Him and hold fast to His church which is the environment in which He has ordained our growth to take place. We need one another to push each other to Christ and to warn each other of false teaching. Together we are called to grow in grace and in truth.

We need the truth of who Christ is and who we are in Him to transform our thinking and every ounce of our being.

How was the Old Testament law and ceremony a shadow of Christ?

_____

_____

_____

_____

_____

_____

How can we guard our hearts from false teaching?

_____

_____

_____

_____

_____

_____

_____

How do we hold fast to Christ?

_____

_____

_____

_____

_____

_____

We no longer belong to this world.

ALIVE IN CHRIST

Colossians 2:20-24

In this passage, the Colossians are reminded of who they are in Christ and compelled fervently by Paul to live in light of their true identity. Paul does not want believers to forget who they are or whose they are. We no longer belong to this world; we belong to God. These verses urge us to live lives that reflect the truth of our identity.

Paul begins with a reminder of the believer's union with Christ and a question as to why they would live as if they were united to the world. Believers died with Christ to their sin and to this world, and we must not forget this vital truth because it transforms how we should live in this world. Paul's writing overflows with references to our union with Christ, and also of the truth that as believers we died or were crucified with Christ (Galatians 2:19). Now our lives are lived not to the old master of sin, but to God. We have died with Christ and been raised to walk in newness of life (Romans 6:1-14). So, Paul asks the Colossian believers why they are still living as if they belong to the world and urges them to view their lives in a gospel-centered way. We are to live in light of who we already are because of Christ in us.

The world's religion and the legalism of false teachers sought to make the Colossians focus on what they did—it focused on outward rules and regulations. But biblical Christianity focuses on the transformation of the heart. Outward actions flow from who we are in Christ. We do not try to conform our outward reactions to a religious standard in order to gain Christ. The worship of legalism and of the false teachings that Paul was presenting was ultimately worship of self. It was a religion of works where a person must be good enough and work hard enough to earn salvation and God's favor. Throughout the book of Colossians thus far we have been reminded that our salvation is not in our own strength, but it is in Christ. The supreme and sufficient Savior that was worshiped in chapter 1 is the supreme and sufficient Savior for our salvation.

It is Christ who is the image of the invisible God and the firstborn of all creation. It is of Jesus that we can say that by Him, in Him, through Him, and for Him all things were created. It is in Him that we have been made alive. There is no need for us to look to the things of this world. Instead we look to Christ who is above all things and through whom all things exist.

The legalism and the religions of the world have only the appearance of wisdom. They may give the appearance of godliness, but they do so apart from any real heart change. True change is rooted in the work of the Spirit in the life of the believer, not just in trying harder and doing more. Ultimately, the false assurance of legalism, asceticism, and all other false teachings will not stand firm. Those things will not be a firm foundation to cling to when suffering and struggles with sin come. These false teachings ultimately place their faith in self and not in God. Paul speaks boldly as he reminds us that these false teachings are of no value.

The gospel shifts our gaze off of ourselves and onto Christ, and that is exactly what the letter of Colossians does. Our hope is not found in who we are or what we do. Our hope is found in who He is. We cling to Christ and nothing else, and we must remember as we face this life that our hope is not found in ourselves, but in Christ alone.

True change *is rooted in the work of the Spirit in the life of the believer, not just in trying harder and doing more.*

How should our identity in Christ change the way that we live?

_____

_____

_____

_____

_____

_____

_____

Read Romans 6:1-14. What does this passage show you about the believer's union with Christ?

_____

_____

_____

_____

_____

_____

_____

Why is confidence in ourselves powerless to help us or stop us from sinning?

_____

_____

_____

_____

_____

_____

_____

WE ARE
CALLED
TO LIVE A
RESURRECTION
LIFE.

SET YOUR MIND ON THINGS ABOVE

Colossians 3:1-2

———

Who are we to be in light of salvation? We know that we have died to sin and been made alive in Christ, but what does that mean for our everyday lives? How does union with Christ transform our everyday moments? Paul has spent two chapters pointing us to Christ and teaching us who He is. He has reminded us that we have died to sin, and he has warned us against false teachings that would seek to add to the finished work of Christ. We have seen who Christ is and who we are in light of who He is. Now we see the imperative that follows the indicative. After learning who we are in Christ, we now learn how we should live in Christ.

Just as we were crucified with Christ, we have also been raised with Christ. Now we are called to live a resurrection life. We are called to live lives of holiness because we are in Christ. Through our union with Christ, we are united to Him in His death. At the cross, we died to sin and to the old way of life. Now, through His resurrection, we are raised to new life. We are raised in Him and He is in us. This passage is a beautiful illustration of the already/not yet of our faith. Already, we are raised with Christ through our union with Him and called to live in light of that resurrection, and yet we also await a final resurrection in eternity. We await resurrection, and yet we have already obtained it. Now we live as a reflection of the new life that is ours in Christ.

We are called to seek the things which are above. But where is above? This does not merely refer to the things in heaven, but to our Savior in heaven. Paul alludes to Psalm 110:1, from the most often quoted psalm in the New Testament, to remind us that Jesus is in heaven. Heaven is not wonderful because of streets of gold; it is wonderful because of Jesus. So when Paul calls us to seek the things above, He

———

is calling us to set our hearts and fix our gaze on Jesus. We look upon Him. We remember His life. We fix our eyes upon His character. We seek Him with our whole heart, not out of some strength or goodness in ourselves, but as an overflow of gratitude to the One who has sought us first.

Seeking the things of Christ is seeking to be holy as He is holy. Perhaps as Paul commanded for us to seek the things of Christ, he was thinking of the character traits that he would list later in the chapter in Colossians 3:12-17, or of the things that he commanded the Philippian believers to think on in Philippians 4:8. These virtues and character traits are not simply moral objectives for us to achieve, but they are the character of Jesus that we are to imitate. Through our union with Christ, they are who we truly are as well. Paul asks that we live in light of our resurrection with Christ and our identity in Him.

We are then told to set our minds on these things. This is not simply to think about these traits as an academic exercise, but to fix our will on them and allow our thinking to be transformed by Jesus. We are to intrinsically be tied to Christ and united with Him so that His focus becomes our focus, that His goals become our goals, and that little by little our heart, mind, and will is shaped by who He is. Our union with Christ must shape our every moment as a child of God. The Christian life is one of constant recalibration of our thinking to the mind of Christ.

What does this mean for our struggles, our sufferings, and the everyday mundane of life? It means that we have a new perspective on every moment. It means that though some days we are tempted to get stuck in the here and now, to struggle with our sin, and to be discouraged by temporary struggles, we can recalibrate our thinking to the mind of Christ. It means that we can live with eternity in mind. We can focus on what matters and trust God with the daily anxieties that will soon be forgotten. And for the deep sufferings and heavy pain that weigh on our souls, we can run to Jesus knowing that He has conquered all sin, suffering, and pain on the cross and through the power of the resurrection. We can preach the gospel to ourselves and remember that just as He has been raised, we have been raised as well. We can remember that resurrection life is not something that God desires for us someday, but that we can walk in right now — not in our own strength, but in union with Christ. Day by day we can come to His Word and ask Him to align our hearts, minds, and wills with His own. And day by day and moment by moment, we can be confident that He will do it.

What are "the things above" that Paul references?
Colossians 3:12-17 and Philippians 4:8 may provide you some guidance.

_____

_____

_____

_____

_____

What are the "things of this earth"?

_____

_____

_____

_____

Why are we tempted to focus on the things of this earth?

_____

_____

_____

_____

What are some practical ways that you can set your heart, mind, and will on Christ this week?

_____

_____

_____

_____

_____

COLOSSIANS 3:15

And let the peace of Christ,
to which you were also called
in one body, rule your hearts.
And be thankful.

WEEK FOUR REFLECTION

Paraphrase the passage from this week.

_____
_____
_____
_____
_____
_____
_____
_____

What did you observe from this week's text about God and His character?

_____
_____
_____
_____
_____
_____
_____
_____
_____

What does this passage teach about the condition of mankind and about yourself?

_____
_____
_____
_____
_____
_____
_____

How does this passage point to the gospel?

_____
_____
_____
_____
_____
_____
_____
_____
_____

How should you respond to this passage? What is the personal application?

_____
_____
_____
_____
_____
_____
_____
_____
_____
_____

What specific action steps can you take this week to apply this passage?

_____
_____
_____
_____
_____
_____
_____
_____
_____

OUR UNION

WITH CHRIST

MUST CHANGE

THE WAY THAT

WE LIVE.

CHRIST WHO IS OUR LIFE

Colossians 3:3-4

———

Set your heart and mind on things above. This is the command that has been given to us. Now in these verses, Paul reminds us again of why we are to do this. Whenever Paul gives an imperative, he provides for us the theological reasoning behind it. These are not empty commands that Paul gives, but commands that are rooted in the truth of who we are and who God is.

We are reminded again that we have died. The people of God have died to their sin that once enslaved them. They have died to the old man and the old way of life and have been raised with Christ as we learned in Colossians 3:1. From being dead in sin to now being alive in Christ, our position and location have changed because of what God has done. We can almost hear Paul urging us to remember who we are because of who He is. It is an urgent tone that will continue in the coming verses as we are commanded to put our sin to death. Our union with Christ must change the way that we live.

Verse 2 speaks of believers being hidden in Christ. Our location has changed, and yet it is right now out of view from the world around us. We still look the same as everyone else, but something drastic has changed within us. The word hidden also gives us a strong sense of our security and safety in Christ. We see this same wording used in the Old Testament in passages like Psalm 27:5-6, 31:19-20, and Isaiah 49:2. We are safe and secure in this new position. The people of God will persevere not because of some hidden strength of their own, but because they are hidden with Christ in God.

God's people will persevere until the day when the heavens open and Jesus returns. Even here in verse 4, we are reminded of the glorious Christology of Colossians. Christ is our life. He is everything. And our

———

hearts yearn for the day of His appearing. We long for the day when what we shall be will be hidden no more. We long for the day when we are made complete. We set our hearts on the day that we will be like Him.

Throughout the New Testament, the apostles longed for this day and urged us to look forward to it as well (1 John 3:1-2, Romans 8:18-39). This hope is certain and sure. Romans 8:29-30 echoes the certainty of the resurrection and appearing of the Christian that Paul speaks of here. In those verses, Paul speaks of various aspects of salvation, and when he speaks of the believer's final glorification, he does so in the past tense. Our future is as certain as if it had already happened. The end of our story has already been recorded, and we look forward in hope to the day that it will be accomplished just as He has said. His promises will not fail us.

We await the day when we will be what he has declared us to be (justification). And on that glorious day when we see the face of Jesus, we will be (glorification) what little by little He has been making us to be (sanctification).

For now we live in our time of sanctification. We are being made holy, just as He has already declared us to be. We are being formed into the image of Christ. We are learning to put away our sin and cling to Christ. We live in the truth of 2 Corinthians 3:18. We behold our God through His Word and we are being transformed into the image of Christ from one degree of glory to the next. The process of sanctification is not one that happens immediately or all at once, but in the life of every child of God, it is always happening. One degree at a time we are being made holy. It may not seem noticeable at first, but it is happening. Like being outside on a cool day as the temperature slowly raises one degree to the next. At first we barely notice the change, but eventually we realize that Spring has come — one degree to the next. One small bit of growth in holiness day by day adds up to a life that has been transformed by the faithfulness of God.

We do not hold out with wishful thinking for the day of His returning. We await that day with confident expectation in the faithfulness of God. We live in hope. We are in Christ as Colossians 1:27 reminded us, and He is our hope of glory. Our future is certain, and His promises are true. Now we must live in light of that glorious truth.

———

We behold our God through His Word.

Why do you think Paul reminds us of our position in Christ? How does this impact the way that we think and live?

_____

_____

_____

_____

What is the hope of the believer?

_____

_____

_____

_____

Read 1 John 3:1-2 and Romans 8:18-39. How do these passages help you to understand what we are waiting for?

_____

_____

_____

_____

Read 2 Corinthians 3:18. How is God growing you right now to be more like Him? Pray that He will continue to shape your life into His image.

_____

_____

_____

_____

Live like who you are.

PUT SIN TO DEATH

Colossians 3:5-8

———

*Dear Child of God, you have died with Christ. You have been raised
with Christ. You are united to Christ. Now live like who you are.
Live in accordance with who He has made you to be. You are new
and no longer what you once were. Live like it is true.*

Paul's command is a strong one that comes on the heels of the hope of
the believer. We have hope because we are His. He is in us and we are
in Him. Now in light of who we are in Christ, we are called to grow in
holiness and shun the sin that characterized our life apart from Christ.
The command for every believer is to put sin to death. Not even one
speck of sin should be tolerated, instead of every ounce of ungodliness
in word, deed, or thought should be eradicated from the believer's life.

Paul speaks of putting sin to death. The theological principle is called
mortification, and it is essential to holiness. We do not grow in grace and
in godliness by pretending that we do not struggle with sin. Instead, we
actively and offensively fight the sin that rises up in our flesh. Believers
are called to be focused on the things above which are the things of
Christ. So, it is easily understood why the command here is to put away
what is earthly in us. We are children of another kingdom, so we must
live in light of the kingdom of God and not the kingdom of this world.

In this passage, we see a lengthy list of sins provided. Though the list is
not exhaustive, it summarizes so much of the sin that we battle in the
Christian life. Paul begins with sexual immorality. This is any sexual ex-
pression outside the bond of biblical marriage. It is not difficult to see
in our culture the myriad of ways that sexual immorality is expressed,
and sadly it is prevalent both outside and inside the church. But Paul
does not stop with the blatant and outward forms of sexual sin, he goes
further to the root of our sin. He also speaks of impurity, passion, and
evil desire from which sexual immorality grows out of. In much the same
way that Jesus spoke of sexual sin in Matthew 5:27-30, Paul recognizes
that sexual sin is simply an overflow of sins of the heart. It is of these
sins both outward and inward that we are commanded to flee.

———

Covetousness is next on the list, and though some may think of it as a lesser sin compared to some that Paul names, it is this sin that Paul reminds us is idolatry at its core. In actuality, all sin at its core is a form of pride and idolatry. Covetousness is desiring what another person has, and it is an accusation against the goodness and sovereignty of God. We think that we know better. We think somehow that God is holding out on us and giving good gifts to others while overlooking us. This is an assault on the character of God that is rooted in our own idolatry and self-worship.

Paul warns of the wrath of God against sin, and then urges the Colossian believers to remember who they are. The sin that he is describing should not be their reality anymore. They have been made new by the blood of Christ. The list of sins continues with anger, wrath, malice, slander, and obscene talk. These are all sins that flow from a heart of anger and ultimately a heart of pride. Though at first glance they relate to how we engage with others, they also deal with how we engage with God. This can also be a form of idolatry when we set ourselves as our own god. This is not who we are in Christ, and we must flee from sin's trap.

Put it to death. Flee from it. The language is strong, because the consequences of continuing in our sin are great. But if we are going to put our sin to death and flee from it, we are going to have to remember first who we are in Christ. And then we are going to have to cut off the sin. We can't feed it anymore. We can't pretend that it isn't a big deal. And we can't point fingers at the sin of others while the things on this list rise up in our own hearts. We must run and not stop running. Through the power of Christ, we run from our sin and to Jesus.

Believers are called to be focused on the things above which are the things of Christ.

How can you practically put sin to death in your life?

_____

_____

_____

_____

_____

Look through the list in this passage. What sin found here do you find you struggle with most? How can you fight against it through the power of Christ?

_____

_____

_____

_____

_____

Write out a prayer asking God to help you put your sin to death and walk in your union with Christ.

_____

_____

_____

_____

_____

_____

_____

_____

WE ARE

UNITED TO CHRIST

THROUGH

THE *POWER OF*

THE GOSPEL.

CHRIST IS ALL

Colossians 3:9-11

———

Followers of Christ are called to a new way of life. Paul has made clear that believers are to put their sin to death. The new birth changes who we are as individuals, but it also incorporates us into the body of Christ. We are united to Christ and united to the church through the power of the gospel. The gospel changes everything, and this truth is evidenced as believers are formed into the people of God and day by day renewed in the image of God. We are His and we are made for the community of the saints.

The exhortation to not lie to one another is a summation of all that Paul has said about putting away anger, wrath, malice, slander, and obscene talk. The speech of the believer should be characterized by truth and grace. The reasoning behind the command not to lie is straight-forward. You have put off the old self and its practices. You are no longer who you once were. And even more than that, you have put on the new self. Every part of you is now fundamentally different. Things are no longer the same. All things have been made new.

And while all things in one sense have been made new, there is another sense in which all things are continually being made new. Paul tells us that we are being renewed in knowledge after the image of our Creator. We see here the truth that though salvation is something that happens in an instant, there is an aspect of our salvation that is an ongoing process. This is our sanctification. Little by little and day by day, we are being molded and transformed into the image of Christ. Our minds are being renewed (Romans 12:1-2) through the Word and Spirit of God. We are growing in our knowledge of who God is, and this only happens through the Word of God. The wording of the end of verse 10 calls our attention all the way back to Genesis and the truth that we have been made in the image of our God (Genesis 1:26-27). The words also draw our attention to Colossians 1:15 and the reminder that Jesus is the image of the invisible God. One of the miracles of the

———

Christian life is that we are being transformed into the image of our God. Through every day of our lives and every moment on this earth, we are being fashioned into the likeness of our Savior by the very words of God.

This passage ends with a reminder of the unity and reconciliation that comes through the power of the gospel. In Christ, barriers are broken down. In Christ, those who come from different ethnicities, cultures, and backgrounds are made one. Is it any wonder that a perpetual tool of the enemy is to cause racial division? This is a tool of the enemy because it is the opposite of what the gospel does. The gospel unites those that have a common Savior. Barriers are broken down and restoration is set in motion through the power of the gospel. Paul speaks of people groups that were radically opposed to one another and tells us that there is now no difference. Our identity is not rooted in our ethnicity, our social status, or any other human measurement. In Christ, we are made one.

Not only are we made one in Christ, but we worship Christ together as one. Christ is all and in all. He is the place that we run and the refuge for our souls. He is the One who graciously binds together the hearts of people that are different from one another. He makes us one people. He makes us the church. He calls us to live in light of what He has done. He has reconciled us, and He is renewing us. Now we press on and follow Him together.

——

One of the miracles of the Christian life is that we are being transformed into the image of our God.

Why do you think we are commanded to not lie to one another? How does this command tie in to the commands of previous verses?

_____

_____

_____

_____

_____

The process of sanctification is an ongoing and continual process. How does this process take place?

_____

_____

_____

_____

How does the gospel break down the barrier between people groups?

_____

_____

_____

_____

What does it mean to live in light of the truth that Christ is all?

_____

_____

_____

_____

Through the power of the Spirit, we
are invited to join His work.

GOD'S CHOSEN ONES

Colossians 3:12-13

———

With the reminder that Christ is all fresh on our minds, we are given a fresh vision of what the believer's life and character should look like. Paul has urged the Colossian believers to put off the works of the flesh, to live in light of the resurrection, and to seek after Christ and His kingdom. Paul's earnest pleading in this passage is not simply for believers to be good people or to live a life of morality. Paul's plea is for the church to be like Christ. What we find here is not just a list of character traits that Christians should accomplish, but rather the character of Christ that God is transforming us into.

Through the power of the Spirit, we are invited to join His work. This is the work of sanctification. Though the work of our salvation is entirely a work of God, the work of sanctification is a work of God that we are invited to take part in. It is the Lord who transforms us, and yet He calls us upward to live in the holiness that He is forming within us. We are called to take off the filthy rags of the old man and put on the clean garments of the new man.

Before Paul speaks of the action that we must take, he first reminds us of who we are. He speaks of the church as God's chosen ones who are holy and beloved. Paul uses descriptions that are common of Israel in the Old Testament as he presents the church as the new Israel in Christ. The descriptions are used often of Israel (Deuteronomy 7:6-11, 14:2), but they are often used of Jesus who is the true and better Israel (1 Peter 2;4-6, John 6:69, Acts 4:27,30, Matthew 3:17, Ephesians 1:6). The people of God are in Christ and joined to the true and better Israel. We are God's chosen ones. We are holy because we are chosen, and we are chosen because we are beloved.

———

Our position as God's chosen ones who are holy and beloved is rooted in our identity and union with Christ. We are holy and beloved not because of any good in ourselves, but because we are in Christ. In the same way, the call to put on these attributes is a call to Christ-likeness. We are called to be like Jesus who is the perfect embodiment of all of these traits. We look to Christ as our example and for the power to grow in these things.

We are called to have compassionate hearts. This is a deep-rooted compassion that flows from the core of our being. The original languages have the idea of compassion that flows from our bowels. In the first century culture, a person's bowels were identified with who they were at their core, their heart, mind, and emotions. Paul is telling believers that at the center of our being, we should be people who overflow with the mercy and compassion of Christ. The next attribute we are called to put on is kindness. This is again an attribute of God and it is the way that God in Christ treats us. He is good and kind to us and we are commanded to be like Him in this way.

The people of God must also be clothed with humility. This is a gospel-centered view of self, and again we look to Jesus as the ultimate example of humility. He was willing to lay down His life and His rights for His people, and because of who He is, we can lay down the pride that holds us back from trusting and serving the Lord fully. Meekness and patience in many ways are the outworking of these first traits. Meekness is dealing with others in gentle humility and patience is humbly responding to our life. With patience, we trust that God's plan is best and with patience we endure trials. With patience we are compassionate, kind, and meek. Verse 13 provides for us a picture of what it looks like for these traits to be lived out. As we grow in them, we learn to bear with one another and to forgive in the way that we have been forgiven.

The fruit of the Christian life is growing in Christlikeness as we continually abide in Christ. A robust understanding of the gospel and how these traits have been manifested to us in Christ, causes them to overflow from our lives as we encounter others. In our attitudes and in our actions, we are called to reflect Christ.

We are holy and beloved not because of any good in ourselves, but because we are in Christ.

Why do you think Paul reminds us who we are before telling us how we should live?

_____

_____

_____

_____

_____

How are the traits listed in today's passage perfectly displayed and demonstrated in Jesus?

_____

_____

_____

_____

_____

Which one of these traits is most difficult for you?

_____

_____

_____

How can these traits be practically displayed in your life this week?

_____

_____

_____

_____

_____

LOVE IS THE
CLOAK THAT IS
PUT ON ABOVE
ALL OTHER
VIRTUES.

PUT ON LOVE

Colossians 3:14-15

———

With the foundation of our identity in Christ that was put forth in verse 12, Paul continues to extol believers about who they should be. He wants them to become who the gospel has already declared them to be. And in these short verses, Paul reminds them that all of the virtues that he has commended to them to put on, should be bound together with love.

Love is the cloak that is put on above all the other virtues to bind them together. And the other virtues cannot exist in their fullness without the love that binds them together. It shouldn't come as a surprise to us that God wants to show us the primacy of love in the life of the believer. During Jesus' earthly ministry when asked what the greatest commandment was, Jesus famously commanded for the people to love the Lord their God and to love their neighbor as they love themselves. Love God and love others. This is the fruit of a life that has been touched by the gospel. The love of Christ compels us to love as we have been loved.

All of the attributes that are listed here in Colossians 3 thrive in the presence of love. If there is no love, these attributes become distorted. Instead of being a performance rooted in selfish pride, these attributes and virtues are to be an overflow of the love that has been shown to us. That love should overflow into a love for the Lord and a love for others as we are reminded just how much God has loved us. True love is demonstrated in holiness and harmony. And where love abounds, peace rules. And where peace rules, gratitude overflows.

Peace is an essential part of the message of the gospel. It is the gospel that brings peace with God, and Jesus Himself is referred to as the Prince of Peace. The theme of Shalom, or wholeness and completeness, is one that is seen throughout Scripture. And in fact, the peace that we have received from God should overflow into peace with other people. Peace should be the ruling theme of our hearts. Peace should guard our hearts (Philippians 4:7) and flow from us. Where the peace of Christ is absent, conflict will be present. So, in the child of God who is filled with the peace of God and walking in the Spirit, there should be a peace between believers. Sadly, we live in a fallen world and conflict is often present. This is why Paul is so careful to remind us of the impact of love and peace on the people of God.

Paul continues by emphatically reminding the church of Colossae that they were called as one body. From different cultural and ethnic backgrounds, and from different socio-economic and religious backgrounds, God had called together His church and the Colossian church needed to be reminded of that truth. We need to be reminded of that truth as well. Even amidst the vast difference present in the people of God, we can live in peace with one another because we are ruled by the Prince of Peace and united to Christ who is our peace. Paul reminds them of their calling and election. Just as believers have been called to be God's chosen ones as we were reminded in verse 12, they have also been called to the body of Christ, the Church. We are called to be God's own, and part of that calling is a calling to the local and global church.

The final words of verse 15 remind us that the result of this love and peace is hearts that abound in thanksgiving. We are to be thankful for our election and salvation, thankful for the love of Christ and the love of the body, thankful for the body of Christ, and thankful that God is transforming us and sanctifying us into these things. Thankfulness should be an essential mark of believers.

As we think practically about the truths set forth in this passage, we must be reminded that Paul is commanding these things to the believers at Colossae because they do not come naturally to our flesh. We are more prone to critical hearts and passivity than we are to true love. And one look at our social media feeds will remind us that even in the body of Christ there is so often a lack of peace and unity. We are so often prone more toward entitlement than we are to thankfulness. But the good news of the gospel is that it brings the remedy to all of these things. They are hard for us, but they are not hard for Christ. So we cling to Him and grow in Him and little by little through that process of sanctification He will grow these things in us.

We can live in peace with one another because we are ruled by the Prince of Peace.

How is Jesus the perfect demonstration of love and peace?

_____

_____

_____

_____

_____

_____

Which of these aspects is most difficult for you?

_____

_____

_____

Take some time to pray and think through how you can intentionally grow in and demonstrate these virtues this week through the power of Christ.

_____

_____

_____

_____

_____

_____

_____

COLOSSIANS 3:16

*Let the word of Christ dwell richly
among you, in all wisdom teaching
and admonishing one another through
psalms, hymns, and spiritual songs,
singing to God with gratitude
in your hearts.*

WEEK FIVE REFLECTION

Paraphrase the passage from this week.

What did you observe from this week's text about God and His character?

What does this passage teach about the condition of mankind and about yourself?

How does this passage point to the gospel?

How should you respond to this passage? What is the personal application?

What specific action steps can you take this week to apply this passage?

THE GOSPEL

SHOULD BE WHAT

SHAPES US.

DWELL

Colossians 3:16-17

———

The gospel is all that we have and everything we need. So in these verses, Paul urges the Colossian believers to be filled and surrounded by the message of the gospel. It is this Christ-centered gospel that transforms our days and our lives. Paul pays specific attention in these verses to the corporate need for the gospel. The lives of the people of God should be a liturgy of the gospel that is constantly reminding us of who God is and all that He has done.

Paul calls on the Colossian believers to allow the word of Christ to dwell in them richly. The Word of Christ is the Word of God and the message of Christ. Most specifically the word of Christ is the gospel. This personal and corporate call is one that should urge us to gospel-centrality. The gospel should be so much a part of us that it dwells in and among us. It should be part of the DNA of every child of God and of every church. The gospel should be what shapes us as individuals and as communities. When we consider these verses in the context of the Colossian church, we are reminded that the Colossians were facing false teaching that sought to add to the message of the gospel. These verses are a fervent call to lift high the Word of God and the message of the gospel. As believers today, we must remember that the problem that the Colossians faced so long ago is one that we still face today. Though often presenting their message in subtle ways, there is a constant push for a gospel that is Jesus plus something. Yet the truth of the timeless and enduring Word of God remains the same. The gospel of grace is the gospel of Jesus plus nothing.

But this glorious gospel was never meant to be a gospel of isolation, instead it is a gospel of community. The church is the gospel community. And the word of Christ that dwells in each child of God must also dwell within the people of God. The church is the vehicle that God has ordained to carry forth the mission of God. This is seen in the proclamation of truth and the encouragement of believers, and it is seen in the private and corporate worship of God and the daily lives of the local church.

———

The gospel informs us, and it should be the message that saturates the preaching in our churches, the conversations between believers, and the songs that we sing to remind one another of the goodness of God and the message of the gospel. We are people who were made to worship. And our worship is an overflow of hearts that have been transformed by grace. Grace changes everything. It changes our message and it changes our song. And the Word of God always leads to worship. Bible study should lead us to worship. Preaching should lead us to worship. The encouragement of a brother or sister in Christ should lead us to worship. The song of the church should lead us to worship. The gospel should lead us to worship. The people of God who are a gospel people should also be a people of worship. And the worship of God's people should spring up from hearts that are thankful and overwhelmed by the lavish grace of God.

But worship is not limited to the four walls of a church building. All of life is worship. So, Paul reminds us that in everything we do and in everything we say, we live for the glory of God. In the greatest ministry tasks and in our mundane daily chores, we proclaim the name of Jesus and live for His glory. We live in His name by carefully considering our ways and only doing things that will honor Him, and we live for His name by living every moment for His glory. We live every moment in worship and thanksgiving. Because worship and thanksgiving are the natural reaction of hearts that have been touched by grace.

The gospel changes our hearts and it changes our days. It saturates every part of us and overflows into worship and thankfulness. And the blessings of the gospel were meant to be experienced in the context of community. Christ has not only joined us to Himself, but He has also joined us to His church. So in our own hearts and in our communities, we cling to the gospel and we rest in His grace.

Our worship is an overflow of hearts that have been transformed by grace.

How do we allow the word of Christ to dwell in and among us?

_____

_____

_____

_____

What do we learn from this passage about the role of the church in our growth as believer?

_____

_____

_____

_____

_____

Why should thankfulness be a central part of the life of a believer?

_____

_____

_____

_____

What role should worship play in our lives both individually and corporately?

_____

_____

_____

_____

_____

Live every moment for the glory of God.

WHATEVER YOU DO

Colossians 3:18-4:1

———

Paul had just given a glorious call to worship that saturates all of life. His vision for the people of God is that they would be a people who live every moment for the glory of God. With this in mind, Paul begins to write of several instructions for Christian households. Household codes were quite common in the first century, and Paul provides for the Colossian church a household code that is thoroughly Christian, and in fact also quite counter-cultural.

Both before this passage and in its midst, the central message that Paul is communicating is much broader than specific roles or functions. The thrust of his message is that all must be done to the glory of Christ and for the Lord. We work for God, not for man. With this gospel-centered vision in our minds, we are presented with a view of the home as a display of the gospel on earth. Family relationships and most specifically the marriage relationship are designed to point to a far greater relationship—the relationship of Christ with His bride the church. The New Testament contains several of these household code passages. Most notably is Ephesians 5:21-6:9. The Ephesians passage is a close parallel to this one while providing more detail. Another important household code is found in 1 Peter 2:18-3:7. All of these passages should be read in their context within the epistles. These are instructions that are rooted in the gospel and the unparalleled freedom and equality found in Christ.

In Colossians, we see the reminder that barriers and distinctions have been broken down in Christ (Colossians 3:11), and Galatians 3:28 even adds the categories of male and female, showing us that in Christ, barriers are broken down and all can come freely to Jesus. Paul roots his teaching in this unparalleled and counter-cultural equality that is found in Christ, but he also speaks to the world that we live in. Though barriers have been broken down, we live in a world of relationships, and Paul instructs us on how to live faithfully as Christians in those relationships.

Paul speaks to husbands and wives asking for them to demonstrate Christian character in their relationships. The attributes that they are asked to display in their relationships are attributes of Christ and attributes that all believers should exercise. The beauty of the gospel and the transforming power of Christ is displayed both by wives through submitting and by husbands through loving (though both also display both characteristics). These commandments were radical in the historical culture. The idea of submission is not one of blind obedience, but willing and voluntarily choosing to serve another out of love. These verses also do not require a woman to obey a husband who is asking her to disobey the Lord. We always serve God above man. In a patriarchal culture, this was an elevation of women. The command for husbands to love their wives was also a radical command in a culture that so elevated the position of men. The parallel Ephesians passage adds even more here by showing us that this love should be so sincere that it reflects the love of Jesus for His bride. And undergirding these marital instructions is the truth that Christ is all in all (Colossians 3:11) and we are united to Him and we are united together in Him.

Paul also speaks to children and to slaves with commands to obey. The command of obedience is not just to fathers as would have been typical, but to mother and father. And the commands to slaves are a reminder to them that this master is just an earthly master, for the Lord alone is their true master. The passage even contains a promise to slaves of an inheritance in Christ. This is again counter-cultural language as slaves were not legally allowed to receive an inheritance. Paul is setting all relationships in the context of one relationship that changes everything. Through Christ we are set free as a new humanity to a new life that is lived in Him.

And in all things, we are reminded that all that we do is to the Lord and not to men. So, we go forward with grace and truth. We walk in obedience and humility. We walk with boldness and we walk as the children of God. Because the gospel changes everything about everything that we do.

We work for God, not for man.

Why do you think that Paul repeats in verses 17 and 23 the reminder that everything we do should be done to the Lord?

_____

_____

_____

_____

_____

_____

How does the gospel change our relationships?

_____

_____

_____

_____

_____

_____

In what areas of your life do you need to be reminded that you serve the Lord above all? How might your daily tasks and relationships change if you keep this in mind?

_____

_____

_____

_____

_____

_____

_____

GOD IS
DELIGHTED IN
*TRANSFORMING
THE HEARTS* OF
HIS PEOPLE.

DEVOTED TO PRAYER

Colossians 4:2-4

———

As we continue in the final chapter of the book of Colossians, Paul is continuing to speak of the way that Christians should live. He is teaching us how to put on the new self and live in light of our new identity. In these verses, we see that one of the hallmarks of God's people is that they are people of prayer. Paul's words encourage us and challenge us to pray without ceasing and be people that live lives that are characterized by prayer.

These verses urge us to be people of prayer. The opening words of verse two are usually translated as "devote yourselves to prayer, or continue steadfastly in prayer." These words have the idea of being persistent, steadfast, persevering, and devoted to prayer. These words should stop us in our tracks as we evaluate our own lives. Would it be said of us that we were devoted to prayer and that we continued in prayer steadfastly? The command is given by Paul because we need to be reminded of what God has called us to. And prayer does not come naturally to us. We are far more likely to depend on ourselves or worldly wisdom than we are to run to God in prayer. But the good news of the gospel is that things do not need to stay the way that they have always been. God is delighted in transforming the hearts of His people and making them a people of prayer. We must look to Jesus who is the perfect example to us of a life of prayer and ask God to give us hearts for prayer.

We are not only urged to be devoted to prayer, but also to be watchful in prayer. As we pray, we must expect God to move and work in our lives and in the world around us. We pray with confidence, not in our prayers, but in our God. We pray and then we watch and wait with confident expectation that God will work. We must remember that God's answers to prayer may not look the way we expect. Every prayer will not be answered in the way that we expect, and that is actually a good thing. Sometimes the best thing for us is for God to say no to our request. Sometimes the sweetest answer to our prayer is a no from a Father who seeks after our good and His own glory. This watchfulness also likely refers to the waiting and watching of the people of God for the return of Jesus. In waiting and in watching we know that all God's plans will be fully and finally revealed on that day.

And all of this is done with thanksgiving. The thankfulness of God's people has been a key theme in the book of Colossians and here we find the reminder again, that God's people should be a people of gratitude. In some ways we can view this verse as a cycle. We pray, then we wait for Him to answer, then we give thanks. But it is probably best for us to see this not just as a cycle, but as three marks of the believer that should characterize us at all times. We should pray with watchfulness and thanksgiving. We should wait in prayer and with thanksgiving. And we should give thanks and wait for God to work and Christ to return in prayer and communion with Him.

But Paul does not stop at telling us how our lives should be characterized by prayer, he also instructs us as to what we should pray. In this passage, he does this by giving a specific prayer request. He urges the Colossians to pray for him and others who are carrying forth the message of Christ. This mystery of Christ is the message of the gospel and all that Christ has accomplished. He asks for prayer for an open door for the word of the gospel to go forth. The wording here is striking as Paul prays for an open door while he is behind the closed doors of imprisonment. But Paul knows, as we should also, that the gospel is not bound by prison walls or prohibitions. The gospel is powerful and alive, and it is sent forth by our God to accomplish its work. These words should instruct us as we pray. We must pray for the gospel to go forth and for God's kingdom to grow on earth.

What does our prayer life say about us? The things that we pray for can show a lot about what is important to us. May we pray for the gospel to go forth. May we pray for our brothers and sisters around the world. Let's ask God to give us hearts so fixed on the eternal and the things that are above (Colossians 3:2), that it is reflected in our prayers. May we be people of prayer whose prayers reflect the heart of God.

What do you think it means to be a person who is devoted to prayer?
Are you devoted to prayer?

_____

_____

_____

_____

How do prayer, watchfulness, and thanksgiving work together?

_____

_____

_____

_____

What do you pray for most? If what we pray about shows what is most important to us,
what does your prayer life say about you?

_____

_____

_____

_____

_____

After evaluating your above answer, what things do you need to pray about more?

_____

_____

_____

_____

We have been entrusted with the gospel.

WALK IN WISDOM

Colossians 4:5-6

———

In yesterday's passage, we looked at the necessity of prayer in the life of a believer and the characteristics that should make up our prayer lives. Today, we shift our focus from going to God, to going to people. As Christians, we are called to both. As Paul exhorted the Colossian believers to pray, he also encouraged them to pray for him and others as they carried the gospel wherever there may be an open door. Paul seamlessly shifts his letter now to urge all believers, in the same way, to carry the gospel to those they meet. We have been entrusted with the gospel and with the mission of taking it to the world. Paul calls the Colossians believers and all believers to live on mission.

These short verses give us great insight into how believers should live and speak according to that mission. We are called to walk in wisdom. The wording here is very close to the wording of Colossians 1:10 where believers were commanded to walk worthy of their calling. Throughout the book of Colossians, we have seen Jesus portrayed as the embodiment of true wisdom. It should come as no surprise amid the calls for believers to live in Christ and embrace their union with Him that Christians would be called to walk in light of that union by living every moment of their lives in the wisdom that comes only from Jesus.

The life of wisdom in Christ is important in every part of life, but Paul here draws our attention to its importance in regard to the testimony of a believer to the unbelieving world. The reputation of our God and of His gospel is hinged to our Christian conduct. This should be a sobering thought for us. Unbelievers or outsiders as Paul calls them are judging the Christian message by the lives of the Christians that they know. It is a sobering thought, and yet it should also fill us with hope that our lives can display the grace that has been given to us. Paul urges his readers to make the best use of their time. As we live lives that put the gospel on display, we must be careful not to waste our moments or our days. Our desire should be that others would see our lives and know that we are believers. We should desire for others to say of us like they said of Peter and John in Acts 4:13 that it was clear that they had been with Jesus. May this be said of our lives as well.

While verse five speaks to our lives and conduct, verse six speaks to our words. We are to speak of the grace of God, and we are to speak graciously to all that we encounter. Every word that we speak should be gracious. Paul doesn't fill this section with qualifiers or reasons that we could disregard this call to gracious speech. The command is for speech that is always gracious. Our words will be an overflow of our hearts. Jesus declared this to be true (Matthew 12:34). So then, if we are commanded to have words that are filled with grace, we must have minds and hearts that are filled with grace. If we are walking in the Spirit and saturated in the Word, then what will come out will be words led by the Spirit and shaped by the Word.

With wisdom and grace, we should be always looking for ways to engage unbelievers around us. As the salt of the earth, our words should be carefully chosen and seasoned (Matthew 5:13). They should adorn the gospel and flavor each conversation. And for every situation and every question that arises, we should be ready to give an answer (1 Peter 3:15). This readiness is not necessarily linked to knowing everything there is to know about every topic of Scripture, though we should be constantly seeking to grow in knowledge and wisdom of the Word. But this should be tied to knowing the ultimate answer to every question is found in a person. Jesus is the answer that this world is in desperate need of, and as His people, we are sent forth with His message.

May this be said of our
lives as well:
*That is was clear that they
had been with Jesus.*

What does it look like to walk in wisdom?

_____
_____
_____
_____
_____

What does your speech reveal about you?

_____
_____
_____
_____
_____

How do these verses encourage you to live on a mission to reach those around you that do not know Christ?

_____
_____
_____
_____
_____

Who in your life can you come alongside to encourage and point to the gospel?

_____
_____
_____

WHERE THE
WORD OF GOD
IS *PROCLAIMED,*
THE PEOPLE OF
GOD *WILL GROW.*

GRACE BE WITH YOU

Colossians 4:7-18

———

We have come to the final words from Paul in this letter to the Colossian church. We may be tempted to skip past this section of greetings and the list of names that are found here but tucked in Paul's final greetings we find reminders of the message of the book of Colossians. It is here that we are reminded again of the grace that is found in Jesus and of the urgency for us to grow in grace and rest in the perfect will of God.

The greetings begin by pointing us to the ones who would be carrying the letter to the Colossians, Tychicus and Onesimus. The descriptions of these men are reminders of the character traits that the spirit cultivates in his people. They are described as beloved brothers; certainly they were beloved by both the Lord and the church. We also see descriptions here of faithful minister and fellow servant, and encourager. These qualities in their lives were qualities of Christ and an encouragement to us to follow in the footsteps of the faithful brothers and sisters who have gone before is and most of all to follow in the footsteps of our Savior. In verses 10-11 we see the names of fellow workers for the kingdom of God—a reminder that this is the ministry of the church—to work together to build His kingdom and not our own.

We also see some of the themes of the book highlighted in this final greeting. Epaphras is described as a servant of Christ Jesus, and we are told of his prayer for the church of Colossae. His prayer is that the people of God would stand mature and be fully assured of God's will. The Colossian church was a church that was growing, just as we all are. And in their journey, as we have seen, they faced false teachers that sought to add to the gospel. Epaphras prayed for them to stand in mature faith. This same theme was listed as part of Paul's great desire for the church in chapter one (Colossians 1:28). This was part of Paul's plan for discipleship, to make the Word of God fully known and cultivate mature believers. We must not lose sight of this in our own lives, and in our churches. Where the Word of God is proclaimed, the people of God will grow. We need the Word of God to be who God has called us to be. Likewise, it is in the Word of God that we can know the will of God. God's will for us is to be mature believers, to grow in grace, and to be sanctified. If we want to know the will of God, we must know the Word of God.

Paul sends greetings to some individuals at Colossae. This extensive list is rivaled only by the greetings at the end of the book of Romans. Paul greets several individuals including a woman named Nympha who hosted the church in her home. He encouraged the people to not only read the letter together to the church, but also to share the letter with the Laodicean church. The last of Paul's greetings is to a man named Archippus and is an encouragement to us all to fulfill the ministry that the Lord has given to us and be faithful right where God has us.

Paul signs the letter with his own hand with a final plea for prayer as he is in chains in prison. And his final word to the Colossians is for grace to be with them. The grace that is found in Jesus has been a theme throughout the book, and in all the life of the believer so it seems fitting that this is how he would end the letter. The contrast between the chains that Paul is in and the grace that he declares is poignant. But isn't this a beautiful demonstration of the life of the child of God. We struggle and we face suffering, and yet through it all we are carried by His grace. We read these final words with hope knowing that Paul is no longer in chains, but He is still in grace. The grace of His Savior has brought him to glory and we stand firm with confidence that it will for us as well.

Colossians has shown us the supremacy and sufficiency of our Savior. It has urged us to mature faith and to lives that are rooted in Him. So, we look to Jesus who is our hope. We are His people, created in His image. By Him, and through Him, and in Him, we will live for Him.

We need the Word of God to be who God has called us to be.

How do these final greetings encourage you and remind you of the message of Colossians?

_____

_____

_____

_____

_____

_____

_____

Think back over the book of Colossians. What themes or truths stand out to you?

_____

_____

_____

_____

_____

_____

How has God challenged you through the book of Colossians?

_____

_____

_____

_____

_____

_____

_____

COLOSSIANS 3:17

*And whatever you do, in word or
in deed, do everything in the name
of the Lord Jesus, giving thanks
to God the Father through him.*

WEEK SIX REFLECTION

Paraphrase the passage from this week.

What did you observe from this week's text about God and His character?

What does this passage teach about the condition of mankind and about yourself?

How does this passage point to the gospel?

How should you respond to this passage? What is the personal application?

What specific action steps can you take this week to apply this passage?

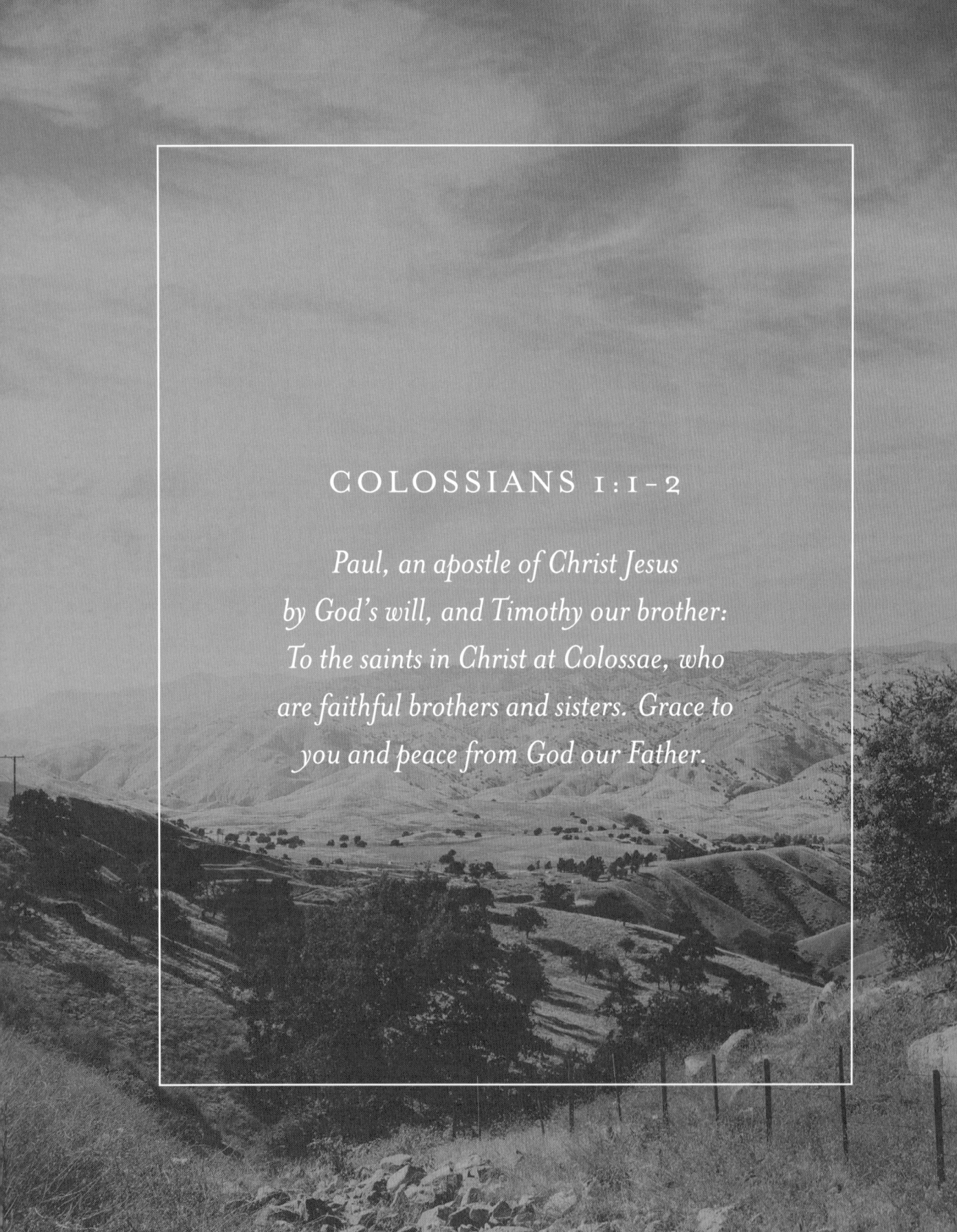

COLOSSIANS 1:1-2

*Paul, an apostle of Christ Jesus
by God's will, and Timothy our brother:
To the saints in Christ at Colossae, who
are faithful brothers and sisters. Grace to
you and peace from God our Father.*

PAUL AND TIMOTHY

———

Paul, an apostle of Christ Jesus by God's will, and Timothy our brother ...

In the very first verse of this book we read two names: Timothy and Paul. Colossians is a letter written to the church in Colossae, and Paul is the author and sender of this letter, but he includes Timothy in this verse. Why might this be? Many of us are familiar with Paul, considering he wrote a large portion of the New Testament, but who is Timothy? And why would he be included in writing this letter?

Paul's introduction is not necessarily indicating that Timothy is a coauthor of this letter, but he is communicating that Timothy was with him during its writing. This is significant for us to deepen our understanding of their relationship and further comprehend some of Paul's later letters to Timothy. Timothy is Paul's protégé, so to speak. Paul and Timothy first meet in Acts chapter 16, where we read that he was the son of a Jewish woman and a gentile man. In Paul's later letters, we read that Timothy was discipled by his believing mother and grandmother. Paul selected Timothy to serve with him on his missionary journeys. It is expected that while serving in ministry with Paul, Timothy was continually learning from the apostle and being theologically trained.

Timothy remained with Paul during his time in Ephesus, and from there Paul commissioned him to leave for Macedonia. After a time, they met again in Corinth, and then in Macedonia. Timothy was with Paul while he wrote 2 Corinthians, Philippians, 1 & 2 Thessalonians, Philemon, as well as the letter to the Colossians. Eventually, Paul entrusted the church of Ephesus to Timothy where he became the pastor.

Paul and Timothy were close companions. Paul wrote two pastoral letters to him toward the end of his own life (1 & 2 Timothy). Paul knew that the mission of church planting needed to continue on, and Paul appointed Timothy with that weighty task. This verse may not seem to add much to our spiritual formation, but in it, we learn that Christian companionship and mentorship is needed in the flourishing of the church.

CHARTING PAUL'S SUFFERING IN MINISTRY
through the book of Acts

Many of us understand that suffering is part of the Christian life and we see that in Colossians 1:24. Looking through the book of Acts and seeing the many sufferings that Paul endured for the sake of the church emboldens us in our everyday lives to live in a way that prioritizes the Gospel and Christ's mission.

COLOSSIANS 1:24

Now I rejoice in my sufferings for your sake, and in my flesh I am filling up what is lacking in Christ's afflictions for the sake of his body, that is, the church ...

①
ACTS 9:15-16
The Lord sets aside Paul as His instrument and reveals that Paul will suffer for His name.

②
ACTS 9:29
Hellenists seek to kill him.

③
ACTS 13:50
Jews incited persecution against Paul and Barnabas and drove them away.

④
ACTS 14:5
The people of Iconium attempt to stone Paul and Barnabas.

⑤
ACTS 16:23
Paul and Silas imprisoned.

⑥
ACTS 17:5-7
Paul and Silas driven out of Thessalonica after a mob formed against them.

⑦
ACTS 18:12
In Corinth, Paul is persecuted by the Jews but is spared by Gallio.

⑧
ACTS 19:23-41
A riot forms in Ephesus against Paul.

⑨
ACTS 20:3
Paul learns of a plot formed against him when he was about to leave for Syria.

⑩
ACTS 21:27-35
Paul is thrown out of the temple because he preached the Gospel. Soldiers beat and arrest him.

⑪
ACTS 22:24-29
Paul is nearly flogged by the Roman Tribune.

⑫
ACTS 23:12-22
The Jews plot for Paul's life and vow a hunger strike until he is killed.

⑬
ACTS 27
Paul is caught up in a storm at sea, and is eventually shipwrecked.

⑭
ACTS 28:3-5
Paul is bitten by a viper.

⑮
ACTS 28:17-31
Paul is under house arrest in Rome.

IN 2 CORINTHIANS 11:23-28
PAUL DETAILS SOME OF HIS HARDSHIPS:

Imprisonment, beatings, near death experiences, lashings, stoning, shipwrecks, robberies,
dangerous people and situations, sleepless nights, hunger, thirst, inadequate clothing,
and daily concern for the churches.

WORD STUDY

ἐξαλείφω | EXALEIPHO | ex-al-i´-fo

———

to smear out, i.e. obliterate (erase tears, figuratively, pardon sin):
blot out, wipe away.

COLOSSIANS 2:13-14

And you, who were dead in your trespasses and the uncircumcision of your flesh, God made alive together with him, having forgiven us all our trespasses, by canceling the record of debt that stood against us with its legal demands. This he set aside, nailing it to the cross.

When you read the word cancel, what do you think of? Maybe canceling a subscription or canceling an action on a computer? The general thought behind this word is to halt or stop. When we read Colossians 2:13-14 in English, we can certainly understand what it means by "canceling the record of our debt," but how can researching the Greek word for cancel, *exaleipho*, help us have a better understanding of the Scriptures?

The word exaleipho isn't a casual word for cancel, like canceling a Netflix account. Exaleipho is more permanent. It is a revocation or eradication of something. When something is exaleipho-ed, it is forgotten, cleaned, and erased. So, when Paul writes in Colossians that our trespasses are exaleipho-ed, he is testifying to the power of Christ's blood to pardon our sins. This erasure of our transgressions is permanent and justifies us. Paul points to the "legal demands" that our sins left us in. The penalty that our sins demand is punishment and death. But by faith in the blood of Jesus, our indebtedness and the price we owe is blotted out, wiped away, erased, and canceled. That is the splendor of the gospel.

Our hope is staked on God exaleipho-ing on our behalf. This same word is used in one of the most hopeful verses in the Bible, Revelation 21:4, "He will wipe away every tear from their eyes, and death shall be no more, neither shall there be mourning, nor crying, no pain anymore, for the former things have passed away." The words translated "wipe away" is exaleipho. In the same fashion that Christ's blood erases our debt, His finger will exaleipho our tears in the new heaven and new earth. He will blot them out, wipe them away, cancel, and erase them. They will be no more.

So, we take heart in God attending to us so tenderly by canceling our record of debt and wiping our tears away. He is a God who sees us as we are—in desperate need of His grace. And He doles out His grace in forgiving our sins and in wiping away each of our tears now and forevermore.

———

MAP OF COLOSSAE

and other noteworthy locations

COLOSSIANS 3:12-17

———

Therefore, as God's chosen ones, holy and dearly loved, put on compassion, kindness, humility, gentleness, and patience,

bearing with one another and forgiving one another if anyone has a grievance against another. Just as the Lord has forgiven you, so you are also to forgive.

Above all, put on love, which is the perfect bond of unity.

And let the peace of Christ, to which you were also called in one body, rule your hearts. And be thankful.

Let the word of Christ dwell richly among you, in all wisdom teaching and admonishing one another through psalms, hymns, and spiritual songs, singing to God with gratitude in your hearts.

And whatever you do, in word or in deed, do everything in the name of the Lord Jesus, giving thanks to God the Father through him.

HELPFUL TIPS FOR
SCRIPTURE MEMORIZATION

- Read the verse repetitively.

- Meditate on the meaning of the verse.

- Instead of just memorizing the words, seek to allow them to penetrate your heart.

- Pray the verse.

- Think about what it teaches you about the character of God.

- Think about how it applies to your life.

- Think about what you know for sure after reading the verse.

- Try writing out the verse to test your memory.

- Review the verses you have memorized often to keep them fresh.

- Keep your verse with you throughout your day to review.

- Recite the verse out loud.

- Memorize the reference as well, so that you know where it is located.

- Look up definitions of words that are unfamiliar.

- Review multiple translations to better understand the verse.

- Set the verse to music.

- Memorize with a friend and keep each other accountable.

- Read the context of the verse to get a better understanding of its meaning.

- Study the verse in-depth.

- Listen to the verse or entire passage on an audio Bible.

- Have fun!

- Challenge yourself!

- Review. Review. Review.

WHAT IS

THE

GOSPEL?